West From Home

T0054580

THE LITTLE HOUSE BOOKS
by Laura Ingalls Wilder

West From Home

Letters of Laura Ingalls Wilder
San Francisco 1915

BY LAURA INGALLS WILDER

EDITED BY ROGER LEA MacBRIDE

HISTORICAL SETTING BY MARGOT PATTERSON DOSS

HarperCollins*Publishers*

The editor's gratitude goes to each person who helped make this trip come alive:

Irene Lichty, late curator of the Laura Ingalls Wilder–Rose Wilder Lane Museum in Mansfield, Missouri; Elizabeth Anderson, who at the time this book was written was with the University of Missouri Library in Columbia; Evelyn Wells, biographer of Fremont Older; and the late Rose Bunch, whom I met in her apartment one floor above Rose's.

For the photographs: the marvelous Raymond Moulin, who as the young son of photographer Gabriel saw the fair; Gladys Hansen of Special Collections of the San Francisco Public Library; Larry Leiurance and Rene Casenave of the San Francisco Examiner; and the J. Nielson Rogers family, who now live where Laura stayed with Rose.

Harper Collins® 📖®, Little House®, and Harper Trophy® are trademarks of Harpercollins Publishers Inc.

West From Home
Letters of Laura Ingalls Wilder
San Francisco 1915
Copyright © 1974 Little House Heritage Trust
For information address HarperCollins Children's Books, a division of HarperCollins Publishers, 195 Broadway, New York, NY 10007.

Library of Congress Catalog Card Number: 73-14342
ISBN 0-06-024110-1
ISBN 0-06-440081-6 (pbk.)

Visit us on the World Wide Web!
www.littlehousebooks.com

22 BRR 35

To Abby
Laura's great-great-granddaughter by double adoption

"SAN FRANCISCO, THE CITY LOVED ROUND THE WORLD"*

Visitors have been falling in love with San Francisco—"Everybody's Favorite City"—since the Gold Rush of 1849. On two sides the forty-four-square-mile peninsula is framed by San Francisco Bay, one of the more beautiful natural harbors of the world, and on the third side by the Sundown Sea, as native Costanoan Indians called the Pacific Ocean. In Laura Ingalls Wilder's time, much of the fourth side was the Sutro Forest, a great stand of eucalyptus trees planted by schoolchildren.

*The motto chosen for San Francisco's Panama-Pacific International Exhibition.

Then, as now, the homes of San Francisco seemed to be flung across her forty-two hills like wash drying in the sunlight. By night, either misty fog swirled around the streetlights or the skies were so clear that, as a poet of the time, George Sterling, wrote, "At the end of her streets are stars." It was an eager, energetic young city that had proved itself. Tried by the devastation of the Earthquake and Fire of 1906, it had rebuilt itself within six years.

Add to this paragon of places a fantasy world of towers, palaces, obelisks, courts, gardens, sculpture, and fountains along a flat two-mile stretch of waterfront. This was "The Dream City," the Panama-Pacific International Exposition. It celebrated the completion of the Panama Canal, opening world trade for the West. Lavish pavilions from twenty-eight nations were constructed. Works of art were gathered from all over the world. Thirty of the forty-eight states recreated their proudest architecture on the grounds. Illinois and Ohio built replicas of their capitols. Texas reproduced the Alamo. New Jersey re-created the Trenton Barracks, where George Washington had made his headquarters. Oregon, not to be outdone, built a replica of the

Parthenon of Athens from Douglas-fir logs. There were ten great palaces, the most lavish devoted to fine arts. There was a Tower of Jewels in which 135,000 specially-cut prisms had been inset. It sparkled by day with all the colors of precious stones and by night came alive with two hundred hidden searchlights. There were auditoriums, festival halls, and incredible gardens created by John McLaren, best known for his work on Golden Gate Park. And for fun, there was the Zone, encompassing sixteen city blocks devoted to fun, rides, and games.

Jules Guérin, the finest colorist among painters of his time, was chosen to select the colors of the Exposition. He gave the romantic buildings the hues of sky, bay, and mountains, "varying from deep green to tawny yellow, and the morning and evening light." According to the official report, "He worked too with an eye on those effects of illumination that would make the scene a fairyland by night, utilizing even the tones of the fog." Electricity was still a new toy to the world. People marveled when on February 20, 1915, President Woodrow Wilson flipped an electric switch across the continent in Washington and turned on the lights for the first time in the Exposition.

This seemed a minor feat compared to the spectacle of lights that played nightly at the Exposition. These have been compared to the Aurora Borealis. Dances of lights and fireless fireworks came from a scintillator located in the Bay. Before the lights winked out, building by building, after midnight on December 4, 1915, eighteen million eager visitors had poured through the gates. (Ten million had been the most optimistic forecast.)

Among them was Laura, visiting her journalist daughter, Rose Wilder Lane, darling of Fremont Older's lively daily, the *Bulletin*. Laura arrived late in August to spend two months on the crest of Russian Hill, long a haven for writers, painters, and architects. From it she could see and walk to Chinatown, Downtown, North Beach, Fisherman's Wharf, Nob Hill, the Ferry building, and that eminence that Will Irwin called "crazy owld, daisy owld Tellygraft Hill."

The house Rose lived in on Vallejo Street was designed by Willis Polk, architectural director of the Exposition, for himself. One could walk a hundred feet from it to a balustrade to watch the Oakland and Berkeley ferries, trailing their peacocks' tails of white lights, as they coursed back and forth to the Exposition. At the other end of the same block Laura could watch the flyer Art Smith as he circled the Exposition buildings, swooping between the sparkling rays of the Tower of Jewels. Backing it all were the trees of the Presidio, framing the magnificent dome of the Palace of Fine Arts. Bernard Maybeck created this building, the choicest in the Exposition, from Brocklin's melancholy painting "Island of the Dead." (This romantic structure, with its reflecting pool, was so loved by the people of San Francisco they refused to let it fall to ruins as was originally planned. In the nineteen sixties an admirer, Walter Johnson, spent 2.3 million dollars from his own funds for its preservation. It now houses a museum, The Exploratorium.)

It is not surprising that one of the first things Laura and her daughter did was to go for a walk. San Francisco was then, and is now, a joy to walk around in. Indeed the deciding factor in choosing a site for the Exposition was that "it was within easy walking distance of everywhere in the City."

Opening day, the people of San Francisco rose early to "walk to the grounds and to stand, an avalanche of humanity waiting for the gates to part," wrote Inez Haynes Irwin, a well-known essayist. Among them was Mayor "Sunny Jim" Rolph, a South of Market boy who never ceased to be a man of the people.

The official guide to the Exposition suggested, "To walk the long esplanade on the bay shore, the blood quickened by strengthening ocean airs, to rest in the balmy sunshine of the sheltered courts, to traverse the miles upon miles of enchanting aisles in the exhibit palaces in perfect physical comfort, will be one of the cherished experiences of a visit to the Panama-Pacific International Exposition."

Walking had brought about one of Rose Wilder Lane's early journalistic triumphs (a series of interviews with prune and apricot growers she met as she traveled through the now-vanished orchards of Santa Clara Valley). Walking was the thing to do. Small wonder that she and her mother should walk about Land's End, Sutro's, and Ocean Beach. Many weekends twenty thousand people would take the little ferries and Cliff House railroad out to Land's End, to stroll in this scenic area.

When Laura was here, she looked beneath the surface to wonder if the City were truly prosperous. It was. Here and there the bones of the old City—"The City That Was"—exposed by the great leveler, the '06 Quake and Fire, still showed through. There were occasional vacant lots enclosed by rusting wrought-iron fences. In some were marble steps, leading up into thin air. Inez Irwin described them as "a little like meeting a ghost in a crowded street." It may well have been these vestiges of earlier hardship that gave Laura pause, for Quake or no, San Francisco was actually the wealthiest city on the West Coast and fifth wealthiest in the nation. The silver mines of the Comstock lode had made that happen. Laura's speculation could also have been prompted by the simple austerities of World War One. This war threatened the Exposition itself, until daring men went to Europe and brought back the art treasures to be shown. Their effort was worth it. Exposition-goers loved the paintings and sculpture.

Two of the American works, "End of the Trail" and "Pioneer Mother," have since become world-famous. But in 1916, they represented two things—a recognition of the achievement of the westering Conestoga wagons of sixty-five years before, and the culture for which the West was hungry. It was a lovely combination of ideas, embodying an appreciation of vitality, courage, and enterprise.

It was the same spirit that inspired the whole city the night the Exposition ended, as Inez Irwin reported, "to stay for the closing ceremonies until midnight, and then without even picking a flower from the abundance they were abandoning, silently and sorrowfully to walk home."

Margot Patterson Doss
Russian Hill, San Francisco

INTRODUCTION

Tumbled in a cardboard box along with old recipes, faded pictures, and newspaper clippings of persons and events long gone, I found these letters and postcards from Laura Ingalls Wilder to her husband, Almanzo. The first few were addressed in pencil to Mr. A. J. Wilder, Mansfield, Missouri, on envelopes with the two-cent first-class stamp imprinted upon them by the U.S. Post Office. The later ones were mostly in envelopes bearing the return address "The *Bulletin*, San Francisco," addressed by typewriter, and personally stamped.

Laura was always frugal. The writing paper

she used was inexpensive and unlined. It wouldn't take ink, so she used her soft pencil. In San Francisco she sometimes typed on the cheap yellow typewriter paper used by her daughter Rose as a newspaper reporter. The whole bundle of letters was tied with a short length of thin white grocery-store string that had sawn through the crumbling edges of the envelopes over the years. Either Manly or Laura had put them all together in a safe place for looking-at in years to come.

After Laura's death in 1957, Rose in her grief sifted through her mother's papers and tossed into cartons those things that she thought she might want to look at later. But she was never able to bring herself to do so. Then, when Rose died in 1968, I, as her friend and executor, had the task of going through her papers. I had much the same feeling, and it wasn't until recently that I really wanted to read those things that I had set aside. It was then that I opened the carton.

As readers of her Little House books know, Laura was a pioneer girl who traveled throughout the Midwest during her growing-up years. She married Almanzo in 1885 and they homesteaded near De Smet, Dakota Territory. Storms, fire, plagues of locusts, and drought finally forced them to seek a new start in Mansfield, Missouri—"The Land of the Big Red Apple," as its promoters called it.

Life on the new farm was a hard scrabble. During the early years the land couldn't support the small family, so Almanzo took a job selling kerosene for the Waters Pierce Oil Company. Laura managed customer billing and accounts payable, to free Almanzo to do whatever work was necessary at the farm. Eventually, the farm began to prosper and their lives became increasingly happy. Their only child, Rose, recalled the scene later:

At night I took a book home from school, and after supper Papa would pop a big pan of popcorn and Mama Bess [Laura, whose middle name was Elizabeth, was called that within her family to avoid confusion with Almanzo's sister Laura] would read aloud while he and I ate it. She sat beside the table with the lamp on it. Her hair was combed back smoothly and braided in a heavy braid and the lamplight glistened on it.

Papa [whom Laura called Manly] sat on the other side of the table, the pan of popcorn between his knees, and ate slowly and methodically, kernel by kernel. He liked to look at the shape of each one; he often remarked that no two were alike and yet they were all pretty. It was the cosy, comfortable hour for all of us. We had had supper, the room was warm, we were alone together, the horses fed and sleeping in the barn, nothing to worry us till tomorrow, and Mama Bess was reading. That was best of all.

Rose's success in later life—she was a world-famous author before her mother was known outside the Ozarks—was in no small part testimony to the character and intelligence of her parents. She went to work first as a telegrapher for Western Union, then as one of the first real estate saleswomen in California, and in 1914 was a feature writer for the San Francisco *Bulletin* under the tutelage of that great American editor Fremont Older.

By this time she was married, brimful of early success, and eager to share her joys with her mother. She had previously urged her mother to come west to San Francisco but the plans had not materialized.

Now, in 1915, the great World's Fair, called the Panama-Pacific International Exposition, was scheduled to open in San Francisco to celebrate the completion of the magnificent canal through Panama. This was to be a splendid spectacle to show the world that California had truly come into its own in every way.

Rose was eager to have her mother come out to visit her in this, of all years. Rose's letter inviting her mother is undated, and to settle details there must have been correspondence, since lost, between that and Laura's first letter. One problem was having both Laura and Manly leave the farm—someone had to stay home to run it. Generous to a fault as always, and perhaps at heart more of a farmer and less of a traveler than Laura, Manly insisted that she go, and she did. But not without promising that she would be Manly's eyes across the western United States and at the Fair, much as she had been the eyes for her blind sister, Mary, in her childhood.

Thanks to that arrangement we can almost go back in time to an era that would otherwise be forever veiled to most of us. We share a transcontinental train trip with the pioneer girl who first crossed the plains in a covered wagon;

we savor her reactions to the likes of Henry Ford and Charlie Chaplin, and we marvel with her at the ocean, San Francisco's Chinatown, aerial acrobatics, and above all the great Fair.

The sun is shining again in the summer of 1915, and here they are: Laura just turned forty-eight, and her twenty-nine-year-old daughter, in an adventure for them and for us.

Roger Lea MacBride
Miami Beach, Florida

ON THE WAY

In the spring of 1915 Laura's only daughter Rose wrote to her on the stationery of the newspaper for which she was a reporter.

The *Bulletin*
San Francisco, Calif.

Mrs. A. J. Wilder
Rocky Ridge Farm
Mansfield, Missouri

Dearest Mama Bess—

I simply can't stand being so homesick for you any more.

You must plan to come out here in July or, at latest, August. You've simply GOT to, so let me hear no argument about it. I know how you felt about being disappointed before, because I felt every bit as bad, I guess badder, because I was terribly disappointed for myself and twice as disappointed for you, and sore besides because I could not manage better. But this time I am quite sure it can be managed. Unless something very catastrophic happens, like war, or another earthquake, or something.

It won't be as I planned to have you out, because we haven't the machine [automobile] now, and both Gillette [Rose's husband] and I are working, and there isn't so awfully much money. But we can have a pleasant time together, anyway. You can see San Francisco and the Fair, and meet my friends, and we can play together all the time that I'm not working. I have worked this job into a sort of movable feast, so that I don't have to be in the office any regular hours, and you can go with me on lots of my outside work—I can arrange for you to have an aeroplane flight* if you like, and we can eat in all the little interesting restaurants.

I have it figured out that sometime in July I will be able to send you the fare, and while you are here and maybe right along afterward I can send you $5 a week to make up for what

*Rose had by then flown over San Francisco Bay strapped to the wing of Lincoln Beachey's plane—the same Beachey who was killed very early during the 1915 Exposition. He was the first American to loop the loop. Young Art Smith was his replacement at the Fair. The insert includes a photo of Smith looping, while trailing smoke, to thrill the crowd. For the *Bulletin* Rose was doing a series on Smith's life, which was later reprinted as a paperbound book. The few copies surviving today are collectors' items.

you will lose in chickens, etc., by the trip.* I should think by that time all the little ones would be out of the way, and there wouldn't be so much work with them. The strawberries will be gone, and the pressure of work won't be so bad. You will miss most of the very hot weather, too.

I think by getting away from it all for awhile, and playing around with a bunch of people who are writing and drawing and otherwise being near-artists, you will get an entirely new viewpoint on things there, and be able to see a lot of new things to write when you go back. If the farm-paper market is closed, there are scads of other markets open. I got an invitation to submit stories to an eastern magazine the other day which I could turn over to you. I haven't time to write for it myself—it is only a little magazine, but would probably pay $50 or so for a story. When you get things to running so that the farm work won't take up so much time you can do things like that. And with the notes and mortagages paid off and your lovely

*To make up for the financial drain of Laura's not being at the farm.

home all built, you and Papa can take things easier. Next year you can maybe get off and make a little trip together to Louisiana or someplace. The way it looks to me, there are only the debts to clear off and you will have a self-supporting home and can use the little extra sums—the bunches of money, like from the apples or strawberries—that come in, to play with.

Anyway, please plan to come out here in July or August, and get the work in shape so you can leave it for three months.

Don't get any new clothes, because we can get those here, except underwear. Suits and things are as cheap here as there, and perhaps the styles would be different—we can get things in a few days from the shops, and then when you go back your things will all be new to the people there. Bring warm things, because it will be cool here—you will wear a suit all the time except in the evening, and probably most of the time then—we don't dress up in the evening except on a rare occasion like a box-party, or something. I have a wonderful dressmaker, who can whip things into shape and astonish you, so don't bother making over anything, just bring it along. I was thinking maybe your rose silk would be pretty with a black lace over it and some coral beads. If you get anything, get some shoes and slippers from Sears Roebuck—they cost out of sight here. Don't bring any extra hats, because by July everyone here will be wearing fall hats and we can get one here. Bring your furs and warm underwear and gloves and shoes, that's all.

I will not talk much about what we will do, because then you will be disappointed when you get here. But we can visit, and play around in Chinatown together some, and you can meet the people I know, and have an aeroplane flight. And you can get acquainted with San Francisco. I am glad you are from the Ozarks, because everything is hills here. It will be foggy and windy and dusty and gray and you will not like San Francisco while you are here, and then when you go away you will always want to come back. 'Tis ever thus. If you like you shall eat an octopus. I promise that.

What do you think of the Art Smith story? It is going fairly well. What do you think of the "Confessions of a Physician"? I think it is awful rot, myself, but the whole *Bulletin* staff thinks it is splendid stuff. I don't know that anyone else does. I will probably be back on the staff of Bessie's* [women's] page sometime in June. I don't mind, it is a soft snap. I will write her another story and loaf all the time.

> With much love,
> Rose

---

*Bessie Beatty, who had earlier launched Rose's career by persuading her to do some freelance stories for the *Bulletin*.

And so Laura set out. She couldn't wait to start describing what she saw and did for her husband Almanzo. This letter was written during her first stop, at a friend's house only sixty miles from home.

Springfield, Mo.
Saturday P.M.
August 21, 1915

Manly Dear,

I am resting in Mabel's room for two hours while she goes to one of her customers' houses and gives them a beautifying treatment. Then she is going with me to get my hat. I nearly got "licked before I started" this morning [from Mansfield]. They said the train would be half an hour late so I went over to Youngs' and Mrs. Y. gave me a cup of coffee—train ran in in just ten minutes. I ran from Youngs' and around the train and caught it, though it had to wait while John brought my suitcase and package from the office.

I will have to go on without my glasses. Had my eyes examined this morning and the oculist said it would take three or four days to make them to fit my eyes. He said, and seemed to prove it with his apparatus, that my left eye is doing all the work and my right eye is pretty poor. He said my left eye was normal, that is as it should be, but it was a bad strain on it to work alone, but the sight of my right eye was all wrong. He says the glasses I should have will have to be specially prepared and that I should wear them all the time to save my eyes, instead of wearing them just when I read, and oh dear me, he says they will cost me $20.

If [Dr.] Fuson is in town I'm going up to see him and find out if these people are all right or if they are on the beat and then I'll know better what to do. I told him I could not wait for the glasses as I was going to California, but if he would keep the record I would see about them when I came back. He said he would do that and if I find I can do no better I can write him and he will send them to me when I come home.

How are you and Inky [their dog] I wonder? The country here is awfully washed. We did not get it all. Was the lettuce seed ruined? Perhaps you'd better look.

Take good care of yourself and Inky and I'll come back before you get to learn how to get on without me. Mabel and I are going out this afternoon and she will see me on the Kansas City train at 10:40 this evening.

With love,
Bessie

———

Kansas City
Sunday, August 22, 1915

Manly Dear,

I just did make my train. Train from Springfield was two hours late, loaded with people trying to get to St. Louis from the south and having to come around by Kansas City. There were fifteen coaches and two engines on the train. I sat all the way with a St. Louis German who smelled of beer and said V instead of W, but he was very kind and treated me to peaches and in the night it got cold and he woke me up, laying his extra coat very softly over me. He was old and gray-headed and a perfect gentleman. I'm going to find everyone kind and all the help I need, as usual. Hope you and Inky are all right.

Love to you both,
Bessie

———

Monday morning, 7 A.M.
August 23, 1915

Manly Dear,

Write me so I'll know how everything is when I first get there. Do you remember the address: Mrs. Gillette Lane, c/o The *Bulletin*, San Francisco, California.

We should be in Denver but we are 198 miles away. Four hours and fifteen minutes late, but trying our best to make up the time. There was a washout last night 400 feet long and 40 feet wide, and while I slept soundly on the safe side someone must have worked like the mischief fixing it so we could cross over. It is queer-looking country, great hills of sand with the grass so thin over it that the sand shows through. Sand cliffs along the river and clumps of willows and cottonwoods along the river but not a tree anywhere else, just the sand hills rolling across in every direction. It must be the big ranch country. Every once in a while there will be a house and a barn and a windmill with corrals near. I can see bunches of horses and cattle farther away and bunches of calves nearer the barns. I counted fifty little calves in one bunch and there have been larger ones.

All yesterday there was only one other woman in the car and she had her berth made up and stayed in it. There were three men. I asked one of them if he knew just where we were and so we got to talking. He is a full-blooded Frenchman and his home is Baltimore, Maryland.

Saw my first sage brush this morning. A dwarf variety. It is in little clumps all over the prairie.

I just saw so many, many cattle—must have been 200 in a big pasture. The range is fenced up, you know. The land is so *flat*. This lawyer from Nebraska says it is *beautiful* and the old Frenchman and I smile at each other. He thinks it looks like a great country but not pretty. I don't like the lawyer chap even if he is a graduate of Harvard as he says. He talks too much with his mouth and takes much for granted. Sat down in the seat with me without being asked. I've frozen him out and my Frenchman has shook him and is talking with a nice boy about the trip out of Denver. The Frenchman is on his way to San Francisco but stops over at Denver, while I go on. He was in Belgium just before the war and saw the Cathedral of Rheims, the one the Germans destroyed, you know, and that famous stained rose window that can never be replaced. He is about 75 years old and has told me of his wife who is a New Orleans Frenchwoman, and his mother who made several trips from New Orleans to Europe in sailing vessels when she was a girl.

The hills have rock tops now and are awfully funny-looking. —I was interrupted here by [a man who] was a cowboy in Nebraska when he was young but is now a lawyer. He is on his way to Snake River Valley in Wyoming where he has a ranch.

The country is growing smooth again. We are past the funny hills. We are in Colorado now. There is homestead land here and rights can be bought where it is already taken for from $350 to $500 for 320 acres. The homesteads here are 320 instead of 160, a new law. It is dry farming or irrigation, as one prefers. A lake of underground water furnishes irrigation if pumped. The country is flat and I can see as far as my eyes will let me. We will be in Denver about noon and I am told I can get [a train] out at three o'clock. I have already missed the train I expected to take. Turned my watch back an hour. Western time now.

> Denver
> Monday noon

Well I missed connections at Denver and am at a hotel near the depot. I can go out at seven o'clock tonight and miss seeing the scenery. I hate to do it but rather think I will. If not I can start from here at eight in the morning. I'm rather tired and I wish I was through with the trip. So far everything out of the car windows has been ugly since I left the Ozarks.

I do wish I knew how you and Inky were

getting along and if Mr. Nall [a hired hand] came. I'm so aggravated about that washout that threw the train late but then I suppose a wait is better than an accident.

Oh, Dr. Fuson said to get me a pair of glasses for a dollar that would magnify so I could read while I'm away and when I come back he'll take me to the oculist that does his work and have him fix my eyes up right. He says those folks are a fraud and Mabel said she thought they were on the beat.

Love to you and Inky,
Bessie

———

Denver, Monday P.M.
August 23, 1915

Manly Dear,

Well, I decided to stay over. I figured it out this way. Rose routed me this way so I could see this part of the country and I might never come this way again. If I had gone on tonight I would have had to take a berth and instead I will pay less for my night's rest here. I am undressed and in my room and I have had a cup of hot tea and some hot toast at half past two so I will not go down again. I'm going to bed and sleep the rest of the afternoon and tonight, and go on fresh in the morning. I will have some sleep ahead and will not take a berth tomorrow, so I will save the amount of my hotel bill here and it will be fun for one day to ride in the common coach and see the people. One travels with their own crowd in a Pullman and does not get a chance to see the people of the country they are going through. So I have figured that by what I save in this way it will cost no more to stay over here, and then I will see the country Rose planned for me to see and get to Frisco the time of day she planned for me to arrive if nothing else happens to prevent.

The country stayed flat-looking clear to Denver but I could tell by the air that we were up high and the engine seemed to be climbing. A man told me that we are just one mile above sea level but the country stayed, as to looks, just as I wrote you in my letter on the train.

They were cutting wheat and threshing,

hauling in from the shocks. I saw some irrigating ditches and some fields of potatoes, and the Columbia River runs among grass banks and looks a good deal like the Missouri, only not quite so muddy. The grass grows so thin on the ground that I could see the dirt through it all the way.

My nice Frenchman, Victor Brun, helped me over to the hotel and after I had been in my room awhile he called me to know if I was resting well and if there was anything he could do for me outside. He is very eager to help me and very much afraid he will presume. He went out sight-seeing so I'll likely not see him again. When I go in the morning I'm going to leave a note with the clerk asking him to Rocky Ridge. He is traveling a good deal now. Says he decided he wanted to see a little of the world before he died. And he might come who knows. I'm sure you would like him. Remember, if you can, to ask me to tell you what he told me about Maryland. I will have so much to tell you I'm afraid I'll forget and it is very interesting. I'm going to sleep now and will mail this in the morning.

———

Hurried away from the hotel so fast this morning I forgot to mail this. Am safely on board train for Ogden, and have the first glimpse of the mountains. Conductor coming, I'll give him this.*

Bessie

———

On the train
from Denver to Salt Lake
August 25, 1915

Manly Dear,

I wish you were here. Half the fun I lose because I am all the time wishing for you.

We passed through the most desolate country this morning—the first desert I've seen. The mountains were around the edges and as the sun rose they showed the most beautiful soft colors. There were miles and miles and miles of sand dunes without a spear of grass or a green thing, only now and then where there

* The envelope containing this letter was postmarked Malta, Colorado.

19

was a tiny ranch and a ditch of water from the river. We are climbing up out of the desert now through the encircling rim of mountains. They are simply frightful. Huge masses and ramparts of rock, just bare rock in every fantastic shape imaginable. They are not like I thought. I had supposed there were forests among the rocky peaks, but there is only once in a great ways a stunted pine. The mountains look like those pictures of old castles in Austria we were looking at, and such wonderful fortified places they would make—such castles could be made on them!

I'll have to wait three hours in Salt Lake— then a ride of an hour to Ogden and there is my last change. Then it is a straightway for San Francisco. The cars are a perfect jam, so overcrowded no one can be comfortable. No sleeper to be had and I'm awfully tired. If I had known what a hard trip it would be I don't believe I'd have had the courage, but still I'm sure I'll always be glad I came. If I make connections I ought to be in San Francisco tomorrow, but the train is late and I do not know how it will be. There will be one more ugly night anyway.

Well, yesterday the acquaintances I made were an Englishman and his family. They live in Ogden and were down to Denver on a trip. He worked in the cotton mills in England when he was seven and until he was grown. He had been a Bryan Democrat but is changing to a Socialist, and the woman votes.*

We are going through tunnel after tunnel.

I saw in yesterday's paper that the Russian fleet the Germans had penned up in the Baltic had sunk eleven German warships with the loss of only one Russian.

I wish I knew how you and Inky were getting along and if Mr. Nall was with you. Hope to hear soon after I get to Frisco. I am too tired to write interestingly so I'll quit.

With love,
Bessie

———

POSTCARD

Salt Lake City
August 25, 1915

Train leaves Salt Lake 5:30—San Francisco train waits for us at Ogden so I'm all right.

*There was female suffrage in Ogden, Utah, in 1915.

San Francisco tomorrow.

Bessie

———

Waiting in the depot in
Salt Lake City
August 25, 1915

Manly Dear,

This is the unhandiest depot I ever saw. I can't buy or reserve a Pullman ticket in the building. Have to go to some number on some street out in the town so I'm letting it go. I'd have to check my baggage and hire a boy to take me to the place, and there is not a red cap in sight. It is 1:15 and my train does not go to Ogden until 5:30 so I'm going to sit here and take notice. Goodness knows how I'll find things at Ogden when I get there at 6:30. I'll likely have to stay all night but it will be the last change, and never again for me. When I go anywhere on the train I'll go the quickest way with the least changes.

It is nice and quiet in the depot after that nasty train. I'm in such a hurry to see Rose I can hardly wait, but I guess it will be Friday before I get there if I have to lay up tonight, darn it. I do hope everything is all right at home. Tell Mr. Nall I said he must keep you and Inky cheered up.

Love to you and Inky,
Bessie

———

On train somewhere in Nevada
Thursday, August 26, 1915

Manly Dear,

Well I'm safely on the last lap of the journey. Was so very lucky as to get a lower tourist berth at Salt Lake and did not have to change at Ogden. Our car was just attached to the San Francisco train, but the ugly D.&R.G. [Denver & Rio Grande] being so late hooked us on to a slow train through Arkansas and we are three hours late. Just sent a telegram to Rose when to meet me.

I crossed Great Salt Lake in the moonlight last night and it was the most beautiful sight I've seen yet. Miles and miles of it on each side of the train, the track so narrow that it could not be seen from the window. It looked as though the train was running on the water. I undressed and lay in my berth and watched it, the moonlight making a path of silver across the water and the farther shore so dim and indistinct and melting away into the desert as though there was no end to the lake. I thought I would watch until we came to the end of the lake, but I was so tired my eyes shut and when I opened them again it was morning and we were away out on the Nevada deserts.

I saw the sun rise on the desert as I lay in my berth and it was lovely. The bare, perfectly bare, rocky mountains in all kinds of heaps and piles as though the winds had drifted them into heaps and they had turned to rock, were purple in the hollows and rose and gold and pink on the higher places. There were yellows and browns and grays and the whole softly blended together. At the feet of the mountains lay the flat gray plain covered with sage brush, with patches of sand and alkali showing. Such a desolate dreary country even though beautiful in its way. All morning we have been going through the desert and now we are where there are piles of loose sand. All the way wherever there is a little spot of green someone is living, or perhaps I should say wherever someone is living there is a spot of green, but not always. I saw two houses and a windmill and one green bush between them. There was a river bottom for a little ways and corrals and cattle and a cowboy in red chaps driving a bunch of horses. We thought we were seeing water off at one side and I asked the porter what water it was. He laughed and said it looked like alkali beds. Then we saw them later close by, miles of perfectly white ground. In places it looked like water and then it looked like snow. There was a little house and corral right out in the middle of one big bed. Not a living creature or a green thing in sight. There was a road out and it looked like a road made in about three inches of snow with dry dirt underneath. Oh, this awful, awful country we have come to now.

This is the desert proper we have read of where people get lost in sand storms and perish of thirst. There are scattered clumps of what I think is sage brush and they are nearly buried in drifts and mounds of sand. The ground between is perfectly bare and covered with loose sand and alkali. The car and my eyes and nose are full of sand and alkali dust and everything and everyone is so dirty. We are all making a joke of it. There is a nice crowd in our car and we all talk to each other and have a good time getting acquainted. One woman talking to me this morning said they live in Kansas City and they are thinking of getting a farm. Want to trade city property. She was very much interested to know all about the Ozarks and says they will come down and see them.

We will get to San Francisco about eleven tonight. I think I have brought you up to date so will quit.

Love,
Bessie

SAN FRANCISCO

San Francisco
Sunday, August 29, 1915

Manly Dear,

As you of course know* I arrived safely in San Francisco. As I walked down the walk from the train toward the ferry, Rose stepped out from the crowd and seized me.

On the ferry we sat out on the upper deck and well in front, but a fog covered the water so I did not see much of the bay except the lights around it. I was so tired anyway and I could not realize I was really here. Gillette met us as we stepped off the ferry and we took a streetcar nearly home and climbed a hill the rest of the way. I went to bed soon and have been resting most of the time since.

It took all the first day to get the motion of the cars out of my head. Yesterday afternoon I went with Rose and Gillette down to the beach. We walked down the hill—all paved streets and walks and lovely buildings—to the car line and took a car to Land's End, from six to ten miles all the way through the city except for a few blocks at the last.

* Laura doubtless telegraphed Almanzo.

At Land's End I had my first view of the Pacific Ocean. To say it is beautiful does not half express it. It is simply beyond words. The water is such a deep wonderful blue and the sound of the waves breaking on the beach and their whisper as they flow back is something to dream about. I saw a lumber schooner coming in and another going out as they passed each other in the Golden Gate. They sail between here and Seattle, Washington. We walked from Land's End around the point of land and came to the Cliff House and Seal Rocks but the seals would not show themselves.

We took a side path into the parks of the Sutro Estate, which has been turned over to the city as a public park under certain conditions as to its use. The lodge near the gates and the old mansion itself were built with materials brought around the Horn in sailing ships about a hundred years ago. We went through the massive arched gateway made of stone with a life-sized lion crouched at each side and through a beautiful park of about forty acres. I don't mean we walked over it all, but we walked miles of it. The soil in these grounds was all brought to them, for originally the surface was just sand. The forest trees were all planted by this first Sutro. At every turn in the paths we came upon statues of stone, figures of men and women and animals, and birds, half hidden among the foliage of flowering plants, or peeping out from among the trees.

The house itself is built at the top of the hill. The whole front and side of the house is glass so that one would have the view from every point. The pillars of the balcony have [Delft] porcelains inset, as do the posts of the stone fence around the house. They are small squares as smooth and glossy as my china, with quaint old-fashioned pictures of children and animals, instead of the flowers on my dishes. Just think, they have stood there for a hundred years exposed to the sun and wind and weather without a stain or a crackle. Close beside the house is a very tall slender building, an observatory with a glass room at the top where the family used to go to watch the ships come in through the Golden Gate. The building is so old that it is considered unsafe and no one is allowed to go in it now.

We went from there out on the edge of the cliff where there are seats and statues around the edge and one can sit or stand and look over the ramparts across the blue Pacific. An American eagle in stone stands screaming on the edge at one side. Two cannon were in place pointing out to sea and there were several piles of cannon balls. I kicked one to be sure it was real—and it was. The winds off the ocean are delightful.

We went down on the beach where the waves were breaking. There were crowds of people there and some of them were wading. I wanted to wade. Rose said she never had but she would, so we took off our shoes and stockings and left them on the warm sand with Gillette to guard them and went out to meet the waves. A little one rolled in and covered our feet, the next one came and reached our ankles, and just as I was saying how delightful, the big one came and went above our knees. I just had time to snatch my skirts up and save them and the wave went back with a pull. We went nearer the shore and dug holes in the sand with our toes. Went out to meet the waves and ran back before the big one caught us and had such a good time.

The salt water tingled my feet and made them feel so good all the rest of the day, and just to think, the same water that bathes the shores of China and Japan came clear across the ocean and bathed my feet. In other words, I have washed my feet in the Pacific Ocean.

The ocean is not ugly. It is beautiful and wonderful.

We went from the beach to the Coast Guard or life-saving station and saw the lifeboat. Then we went to see the *Gjöa*, the only boat that has ever gone around the continent through the Northwest Passage. It is battered and worn but strong-looking still. The ship was made in Norway in 1878 and with a crew of six men and the captain was three years and four months making the journey from Norway through the Northwest Passage to San Francisco. The government of Norway and the Norwegians of California gave the ship to this city and left it here.*

By this time I was tired, very tired, so we took a car back to the city and stopped for dinner at a restaurant. The waiter was an Alsatian, which is a cross between a Frenchman and a German. The dinner was delicious. French bread and salmon steak and tenderloin of sole, delicious fish. I could hardly tell which was the best. Then there was some kind of an Italian dish which I liked very much, and a French strawberry pie or "tarte" which was fresh berries in a pastry shell with some kind of rich syrup poured over. There was music in the restaurant and I heard "It's a Long, Long Way to Tipperary" for the first time.

Believe me, I was tired after seeing all this in one afternoon and we have been loafing all today. We went out on the walk before the

*Roald Amundsen had bought this antique and modified it for use in Arctic exploratory work. He spent several winters in northern Canada frozen in, conducting scientific investigations. In the spring of 1905 he emerged from his winter quarters into open water, contacted a passing ship from San Francisco, and realized that—unintentionally—he was the first to navigate the fabled Northwest Passage. The *Gjöa* was at the Golden Gate Park until 1972, when it was returned to Norway.

house and saw Niles [an exhibition aviator] fly this afternoon. The Tower of Jewels is in sight from there too. Niles flew up and up, then dropped like an autumn leaf, floating and drifting and falling. He turned over, end over end, he turned over sideways both ways, then righted himself and sailed gracefully down.

Christopherson was flying at the beach yesterday and Rose says I shall have a flight before I go home. Gee, if it can beat wading in the ocean it will be some beat, believe me.

You know I have never cared for cities but San Francisco is simply the most beautiful thing. Set on the hills as it is with glimpses of the bay here and there and at night with the lights shining up and down the hills and the lights of ships on the water, it is like fairyland. I have not seen any of the Exposition yet. San Francisco itself would be wonderful enough for a year, but we will begin this week to go to the Fair. You must not expect me to see it all for it has been figured out that it would cost $500 just to see the five-cent, ten-cent and twenty-five-cent attractions.

Rose and Gillette have a dandy little place

to live with a fine view from the windows.* It is up at the very top of a hill, with the bay in sight.

Just here Rose called to come quick and go see the fireworks at the Fair. We put on our heavy coats and went out to the walk before the house and just a little way along it and sat down on a stone curb. The white Tower of Jewels is in sight from there. The jewels strung around it glitter and shine in beautiful colors. The jewels are from Austria and cost ninety cents each and they decorate all the cornices on the high, fancifully built tower. A searchlight is directed on the tower at night to show it off and it is wonderful.

As we looked, the aeroscope rose above the tops of the buildings. It is a car that can hold five hundred people. Its outlines are marked by electric lights. It is on the top of a more slender part and is lowered for the people to

* The Editor visited the house in 1973. It was designed and built in the 1890's by the young architect Willis Polk, for his own use. He later became the Chairman of the Board of Architects of the 1915 Exposition. The house is at the very crown of Russian Hill and commands a spectacular view to this day.

fill the car, then is raised high so they can look down on the whole Exposition at once. They have that instead of the Ferris Wheel. As it rises, it looks like some giant with a square head, craning his long neck up and up. I don't suppose it looks like that to anyone else, but that is the way it makes me feel.

Well, we sat and watched and soon a long finger of white light swept across the sky, then another and another of different colors, and then there was flashing and fading across the whole sky in that direction, the most beautiful northern-lights effect you could imagine. I think you have seen them. Well, this was more brilliant, more colors and *very* much higher on the sky. All the colors of the rainbow and some shades that I never saw the rainbow have. I have used the word "beautiful" until it has no meaning, but what other word can I use? There are forty searchlights producing this effect. Forty men handle them, producing the flashes in a sort of drill, under direction and orders as a drill march is done. It costs $40 a minute to show these northern lights, in salary alone. What the lights themselves cost is not for common mortals to know.

After a little of this, rockets went shooting up the beams of light, burst and fell in showers of colored stars and strings of jewels. The different colors of the searchlights were played upon the [artificially generated] steam making most beautiful and fantastic cloud shapes of different colors after the shower of stars had fallen. I do not know how long it lasted, but at last the flashes stopped and there was left the wonderful Tower of Jewels shining and glowing in the light thrown on it, and the aeroscope craning its long neck for a look down on the grounds.

I will meet some of Rose's friends this week and begin to get a line on things. Rose gets $30 a week now and she says she is saving ten percent of it, absolutely salting it down. She says it is not much but it is making a start. Gillette has worked on extra jobs for the *Call** since he came to the city, which leaves him at times without work but he has a promise of a good job as soon as a vacancy occurs, which is

* The newspaper rival of Rose's paper, the *Bulletin*.

expected soon. Rose says they have $4,000 due them from their real estate work and that Gillette has made an assignment to us of what he owes us, but they do not know when they, or we, will get this money as the men who bought the land are unable to pay it now. The real estate business went all to smash and Stine & Kendrick* are resting till things turn.

I am so glad Mr. Nall came so soon and to get your letter. I do hope you and Inky are getting along comfortably. Take care of yourself and him, and I will look for us both as much as possible.

What a time you must have had with those chickens and that milk. I'm glad the pie was good and the thing to do was to put it in the oven. I hope you did not burn it.

Rose says tell you those fireworks are the best the world has ever known. It costs hundreds of thousands to produce them and they had experts from all over the world at work on them. She says there never was anything like them in the world except those Roman

---

* The real estate agency for which Rose and Gillette had worked until a year or two before, selling land in the Sacramento valley.

candles you got for her the last Fourth of July we were in De Smet. They surpassed them, she says.*

Well, goodbye for this time. I'll go see some more to write you.

Lovingly,
Bessie

―――

San Francisco
September 4, 1915

Manly Dear,

So glad to get your letter and know that you were all right. My, how wet it must be back there. I'm glad we live on the hills. Mrs. Rogers is a dear, and so are you for telling me not to worry and to have a good time. But the more I see of city life the more I love the country, and listening to Gillette talk of the

* In nine of her later books Laura described her adventures as a pioneer girl. At last her parents settled in De Smet, Dakota Territory. Laura married there and Rose was born there in 1886. The Fourth of July Rose remembered must have been that of 1894. According to Laura's diary, published by HarperCollins as On the Way Home, the Wilder family left De Smet for a new start in Missouri later that month.

farming the more sure I am that the law of averages holds here as elsewhere. Such enormous profits can be made on the farms here. Very good, he proves it, but still the farmers are unable to make the payments on their land which shows there is a leak here as everywhere.

Yesterday I loafed all day. I can not stand very much, someway. A little excitement carries me over and the next day I pay. The day before yesterday Gillette and I went to the Fair grounds in the afternoon while Rose wrote on her story. Then Rose came down in time for the illumination and fireworks and we stayed until twelve o'clock. One simply gets satiated with beauty. There is so much beauty that it is overwhelming.

The coloring is so soft and wonderful. Blues and reds and greens and yellows and browns and grays are all blended into one perfect whole without a jar anywhere. It is fairyland. We went through a large entrance gate and were in the Zone, which is a long street of attractions like the side shows at a circus, only of course not to be compared with them as they are simply wonderful. We took a seat on one of the little trains drawn by a motor and rode the length of the one, for it is so far and there is so much walking to do. I am going again to look particularly and then I can tell you about things as I should, but on this first visit Rose and Gillette wanted me to see the Exposition as a whole and get a sort of wholesale impression.

The buildings are built like those of a city and the streets and the four corners of streets form the courts. One goes through beautiful archways in the buildings into the courts where fountains splash and lovely flowers and green things are growing. There are life-like statues and figures of animals and birds. The foundation color of the buildings is a soft gray and as it rises it is changed to the soft yellows picked out in places by blue and red and green and the eye is carried up and up by the architecture, spires and things, to the beautiful blue sky above. I have never imagined anything so beautiful.

We did not go through the buildings, leaving that for a later time, but we went into the

"Forbidden Garden." There was, in the old days near a monastery, a garden where women were forbidden to go on pain of death. This is an exact copy of that old garden. The paths leading to it are dim as twilight from the shrubbery growing close over them and they are a sort of labyrinth, so that one comes suddenly and unexpectedly upon the little garden with its splashing fountain and its green grass and flowers.

I saw the Southern Pacific Railroad exhibit in their building which is a life-like reproduction of California scenes, even to the waterfalls and the blossoming orchards in the Santa Clara Valley.

There is one building and courts that the city is planning to keep for a museum and park.* This is where the most wonderful statuary is grouped along the walk and against the walls. "The Pioneer Mother" is one—a life-size group on a pedestal so one looks up to it. A woman in a sunbonnet, of course pushed back to show her face, with her sleeves

* The Palace of Fine Arts, by the California architect Bernard Maybeck, is still a showplace at the San Francisco Marina.

pushed up, guiding a boy and girl before her and sheltering and protecting them with her arms and pointing the way westward. It is wonderful and so true in detail. The shoe exposed is large and heavy and I'd swear it had been half-soled.

We went to the gate to meet Rose just at dusk and then we watched the dream city light up. No lights anywhere to be seen but it was just illuminated—what is called *indirect* lighting. Then we wandered down the Zone. At the door of every show people were "ballyhooing"—doing little stunts to attract the crowd.

The Panama Canal* is wonderful on the outside. It shows the canal with a warship on guard, and the wireless station which is actually sparking and sending out messages. The water flows into and out of the locks and the scenery is correct in detail, tropic of course, and the sky is someway managed by electricity so that it is twilight and the stars come out. Then they gradually pale and the sky lightens for daybreak and becomes lighter

* This was the featured exhibit of the Exposition.

until it is daylight. They say inside there is a huge relief map and a man to explain it.

We went into the Navajo Indian village, regular cliff dwellings. It is built to be a rocky cliff and one climbs up by steps cut in the solid rock all along the way. After you get up the cliff, there are holes dug into the rock, smaller, or larger where the Indians live, making baskets and pottery and weaving rugs. They all smell like wild beast dens and I did not like to be there. The Indians are very friendly and good-natured.

We went from there to see the fireworks which I have described to you before. Seen at close range they are even more beautiful.

We peeped between the elbows of the crowd and got a glimpse of the Japanese wrestling match. Then we saw the Lantern Parade by the Japanese, which was simply a mob of Japanese carrying lanterns. Little and big men, women, and children marched by carrying Japanese lanterns. Rose made a quick move and I lost her in the crowd. I looked where Gillette had been and he was not there. I started to go in the direction I had last seen Rose and then I stood stock still. I'll admit I was terrified for the crowd was a mob and I did not know my way out. Then a hand fell on my arm and Gillette said, "All right, Mama Bess. They crowded in but I have not lost sight of you a minute. There's Rose right over there."

We went on back to the Zone and went to the Samoan village. Samoa, you know, are South Sea islands belonging to the U.S. There were several girls and men dressed, or rather undressed, in their native costume. The girls had bright silk scarves around their bodies covering their busts and waists—but leaving their shoulders bare, then short narrow skirts reaching to their knees. They wore necklaces and strings of beads and rings. The men wore the short skirts but not the cloth around the waist. Their skin was a beautiful golden color where it was not tattooed and their voices were soft and musical. The girls are very pretty and some of the men are fine-looking. They danced their native dances and sang their island songs. The girls danced by themselves, the girls and men danced together, and the men alone danced the dance of the headhunters with long ugly knives. In all this dancing and singing they never touched each other and they danced in every muscle of their bodies, even their fingers and toes. They were very graceful and I did enjoy every bit of it. At the very last they all sang "It's a Long, Long Way to Tipperary." They all seemed very much pleased with themselves that they could sing it and all smiled when they began. Their singing is beautiful and it did seem strange to see those strange, island people singing the English battle song. They seemed cold, poor things, and when they left the stage wrapped up in heavy bathrobes. They are very pleasant to talk to. Their own real live princess brought them over and they have a chief with them. They live in an imitation Samoan village of grass huts. They are all, men and women alike, covered with tattooing from the waist to the knees—so the manager said—and when I caught a glimpse of a knee it was tattooed and it also showed around the waists of the men above the skirt.

We walked miles and miles that afternoon

and evening and I was tired to death.

I am disgusted with this letter. I have not done halfway justice to anything I have described. I can not with words give you an idea of the wonderful beauty, the scope and grandeur of the Exposition. But I will see it more in detail soon and tell you more about it.

I hope everything is going along all right, and that Inky still keeps his appetite. How are the chickens and the pigs and everything? Truly, I am enjoying myself but I am also missing Rocky Ridge. Believe me, I am glad we have such a beautiful home.

I am being lazy and resting but Rose says it is not expected that one will recover from the trip in less than a week. I do not know why I had to make so many changes. The trains I was on simply did not go any farther and I had to change. Rose says she thinks it must have been because of the increase in passenger traffic.

Love,
Bessie

———

San Francisco
September 7, 1915

Manly Dear,

I have taken tea in a Chinese tea room in Chinatown and went through some of their shops looking at the curious things they have for sale. It is very interesting to walk through Chinatown as we do when we walk down town from Rose's place. There are such wonderful hand carvings of ivory and stone and wood in the windows, beautiful hand embroideries and tapestry. Then there are the fish markets with such large fish and small fish, with lobsters and octopus and stingaree and live turtles and shrimps and funny and lovely fish that we do not know the names of. The streets are full of the Chinese people of course. A good many of them are wearing American dress and are very nice looking people. Some still wear the Chinese costume as it is in pictures you have seen and the children are the cutest ever. I do not like the Chinese food and shall not try any more of it.

We went for dinner to an Italian restaurant in Little Italy, the part of town where the

Italians live. It was a funny little restaurant where we could sit and watch the cooking done and the proprietor himself cooked or waited or did whatever was necessary. His wife waited on the tables and there were other waiters and help with the cooking. The room was full of people eating and not a word of English was spoken except by Rose and myself, except when the proprietor struggled to take our order. Everyone was talking and a group of men got excited and talked loudly at each other. I'm sure they were talking about the war. The food was fine, though I could not tell you the name of it, and it was all very interesting indeed.

I am sure by now you are trying to find the ear spoon, and cannot, so I am sending you a Chinese ear spoon,* toothpick, and a fork to eat with. I am so sorry about Inky missing me so much and I am afraid it will only make him feel worse if I send him a letter! I am enjoying my visit and the sight-seeing so much but still it seems as though I have been away

* To clean out the ears. The Chinese stores in San Francisco stocked them in silver, gold, and jade.

from Rocky Ridge for a year. Do take care of yourself and everything. We are going out to the Exposition to spend the day tomorrow. I am tired today and resting.

What an awful time you must be having with so much rain. Oh, did you see in the papers about Pettirossi* falling into the bay with his flying machine? He was not hurt.

Lovingly,
Bessie

I'll bring you the ear spoon after all. I'm afraid it would get broken in the letter.

San Francisco
September 8, 1915

Manly Dear,

I must tell you of the delightful day I spent yesterday. Rose and I went down town in the morning and Rose turned in her copy at the *Bulletin* office. We had a few errands to do and then we had a cup of tea and some muffins at

-----

* A flier from the Argentine who completed a brief engagement at the Fair.

"The Pig 'n' Whistle"—a tea room. Gillette does not come home at noon so we did not, but took the tea and muffins for our lunch. After that we walked out to the top of "Telegraph Hill."

To reach it one goes through the Italian tenement district where the Italian fishermen live, and goes up a steep hill, so steep that there are cleats across the walk in places to help in the climb. From the top of Telegraph Hill we looked down on the bay and boats and ships of all kinds going in every direction. Away out in the bay we saw what looked like a house bobbing over the water and we watched it until it came close enough so we could see that it was a houseboat being towed by a little tug. Across the bay we could see some of the cities of Oakland and Berkeley. In other directions we could see nothing but water. When we tired of this we went down the hill on the other side to the waterfront, among the docks. Most of the docks are covered and look like long warehouses running out in the bay with ships tied up on each side of them. After awhile we came to an open dock, piled full of lumber. We walked out to the end and watched the waves and looked at the military prison of Alcatraz on the island. There were fourteen sailing ships anchored in sight and three big ferry ships. One coast steamer went out for its voyage up or down the coast and several motor boats went by. This is a wonderful harbor, so large and quiet, with room for so many ships to anchor safely, and such a narrow, well-protected entrance: the Golden Gate.

I watched the water until I felt as though the pier were rocking, then we came back and went on down the shore. We passed two launches from the battleships and the sailors from one had turned their pet black goat out on the wharf for a run. We gave him plenty of room. I was afraid he would not know how to treat women. A little farther on we came to some Italian fishermen mending their nets and when we asked they told us where the fishermen's wharf was and we went on down to it. There were so many fishing boats tied up. Some of them were unloading fish and, oh, I wish you could see the fish. There were great piles of them and they were being weighed and carted away and taken into the fish markets nearby. Some were great salmon that would weigh from thirty to sixty pounds. We could buy one weighing about twenty-five pounds for sixty cents. They told us that they went out to the fishing about three o'clock in the morning and we are going down some morning and see them start. Everyone was so pleasant and gentlemanly. When we could tear ourselves away we went on to the California Fruit Association's cannery.

Before I forget it, though, I must tell you that Gillette saw a fifty-pound salmon the other morning that a man had caught with a hook and line. Some fishing?

Well, we went all through the cannery and my doubts about the cleanness of canned goods from a large plant are removed. I felt hungry for the canned fruit right there. It was *clean*. I will tell you about it when I come. It is so long to write. We went all over it. Everyone working there was Italian and I guess there were a couple of hundred girls and don't know how many men. They were so kind and nice to us and when they could not talk English they would chatter Italian at us and smile. After going through the cannery we walked to a streetcar line and came home. Rose figures we had walked ten miles altogether.

Pitch my letters into the bathroom and when I come I'll look them over and tell you more about these things.

Lovingly,
Bessie

————

San Francisco
September 11, 1915

Dear Manly,

This is just another chapter of my last letter. I forgot to tell you that the highest fort in the world is on one post of the Golden Gate. You see, the ocean comes up on the outside, and between two high mountains is a comparatively narrow passage into the harbor of the bay. This narrow passage is the Golden Gate and the fort is on the mainland side. There is no sign of the fort to be seen. The defenses are disappearing guns, and the fort is the highest in the world. The harbor is perfectly protected for that is the only way in.

From my bedroom window today I counted fifteen ships in sight at one time on the bay. One of them is a battleship and there are three cruisers. There are two other battleships out by the Golden Gate. One of them is the *Maine*.* They are in battle paint, grim and gray. The cruisers are white. When we were out at the beach we saw the fastest mail and passenger ship on the Pacific, outward bound. From the gate in front of where Rose lives one can see nine towns, the smallest larger than Springfield and some of them larger than Kansas City. They are scattered along the stretch of bay which can be seen. There is also a great number of ships always in sight, and three islands—Goat Island, Angel Island, Alcatraz Island. The military prison is on Alcatraz Island.

By the way, if you and Mr. Nall care to read Rose's story, "Ed Monroe, Man Hunter," you may do so knowing that all the stories in

---

* Not the original *Maine* sunk in Havana in 1898.

This photograph of Laura Ingalls Wilder was taken about two years after her stay in San Francisco.

Almanzo Wilder, in the field of Rocky Ridge, 1908.

Rose Wilder Lane, a year or so after Laura's visit to San Francisco.

The Vallejo Street side of the house that Rose and Gillette lived in looks much the same in this 1973 picture as it did in 1915.

The rear of the house on Vallejo Street. Carol Ann Rogers leans out of the apartment window Laura gazed through so often in September and October 1915.

The Ferry Tower's huge "1915" greeted streetcar riders. Once aboard the ferries, they could read the Tower's other message, SAN FRANCISCO INVITES THE WORLD . . . PANAMA-PACIFIC EXPOSITION 1915.

Ocean Beach in 1915. Land's End and the Cliff House are in the background. This was where Laura first viewed the Pacific Ocean and first waded in salt water.

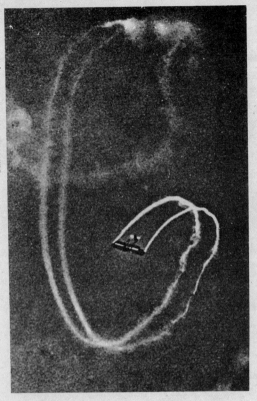

. . . to Loop the Loop, twice!

Art Smith said: "I flew another 500 feet higher, pushed the machine over into a vertical dip, and dropped clean. When I judged the momentum was great enough I rammed the wheel over with all my might. The machine turned completely over, in a beautiful curve. The engine picked up. I had looped my first loop."

> —From Art Smith's autobiography
> written with Rose Wilder Lane

After Lincoln Beachey's death in March, young Art Smith, 21, was engaged as the premier exhibition flyer for the Exposition. Here he prepares to take off.

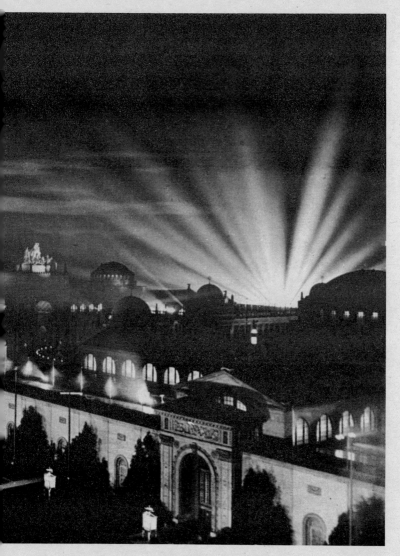

The Tower of Jewels and Exposition grounds at night. "The illumination is gradual. First, the lower bank of floodlights under the palms and shrubbery, next the powerful tungstens in their hooded pillars, finally the great standards flash their millions of candle power full on the ivory façades."

One of the Exposition's most lovely attractions—the color illumination show and fireworks display. Amidst a shower of stars, several of the 40 searchlights produce colorful patterns on steam.

The Palace of Fine Arts, by Bernard Maybeck, is the only part of the P.P.I.E. to survive to the present day.

"The Pioneer Mother" by Charles Grafly was the first monument to be erected in honor of the women who braved the Overland Trails.

A view of the Fair from the top of the aeroscope. The Zone is in the foreground. Seven blocks long, it offered rides such as The Scenic Railway, A Trip to the South Pole, A Submarine Journey; attractions such as the Chinese Pagoda (center photo), a small Celestial City housing a restaurant, theater, and shop; and shows such as Madame Ellis, mind reader, and Captain, the educated horse.

The aeroscope, capable of lifting
passengers 285 feet from its base.

The Court of the Universe from the Tower of Jewels. The *Oregon*, where Rose was photographed with Henry Ford, is on the left.

International Race — P.P.I.E — 1915
Nurdey and Lady Betty.

One of the yacht races held during the Exposition in
San Francisco Bay.

The wharves as Laura saw them, with Alcatraz in the background.

Ferryboats in San Francisco Bay at the time of Laura's visit. One similar to these, on which Laura may have been a passenger, may be visited on the shorefront in San Diego.

An Alaska Packers schooner in the Golden Gate, as Laura saw it.
The bridge was built there twenty years later.

Fisherman's Wharf as it looked shortly after Laura's visit.

Chinatown in 1915.

The running boards on this streetcar make it easy to see how Laura fell.

Market Street, which Laura crossed to get to the *Bulletin* office, located on the far side just to the right of the lamppost in the foreground.

The intricately carved wooden chest Laura brought home with her from the Fair, now in the Laura Ingalls Wilder Museum in Mansfield, Missouri.

Laura and Gillette sight-seeing in the Muir Woods during her visit to San Francisco.

it, although incidents, are true, and *actually happened*. "Ed Monroe" came to dinner with us and told Rose those stories for her to use until after midnight. Instead of being an old detective, he is an old crook who has served time more than once. He was a burglar who did the high-class work, jewelry robberies, etc. He is straight now and working in the circulation department [of the *Bulletin*]. He is very interesting and of course his name is not the one used in the story. He strung Rose's pearls for her, the ones I brought her, you know. He said it was his old trade, the re-stringing and resetting of jewels—when he had stolen them, I suppose.

Rose was much pleased over the little bottle of possum oil and is going to keep it for a curiosity. She has been about sick ever since I came with a bad cold, but I've been dosing her with snake root* and think she will be all right now.

I went down to the *Bulletin* twice with her this morning. We walked down through Little Italy and Chinatown and the Japanese section.

---

* There are many varieties of snake root growing in the U.S., and all have been put to one medicinal use or another. Evidently Laura brought her own and steeped it into a tea for Rose.

It was very interesting and the shops were so full of strange things in the windows. We just walked through so I could see some of the people and get a general idea of it. The old Chinatown is gone, you know,* and the buildings look on the outside like any other. Soon we are going down and rummage in the shops and eat in some of the restaurants, and then I can write you more about it.

Please save my letters. I might want to use some of the descriptions later and I also wish you would ask Mrs. Weed for Mrs. Comstock's address. I was going to bring it with me and forgot.

Gillette has planned to take me into the valley where they raise so much poultry— white Leghorns. It has become current report that the poultry men are not making their expenses, but one man there whom Gillette knows has ten thousand hens on fifteen acres. Three men take care of them and he says he makes $1.38 a year on each hen.

He says the reason the others are not making expenses is because they do not work

* In the great earthquake and fire of 1906.

hard enough, that it takes *Work* to care for hens properly and that they drive in their automobiles too much when they should be working. I want to see how he handles so many hens and I think I'll get a chance to go.

Have you turned the hogs into the orchard yet and did they like it? Will they leave the green feed and come up for their dose of medicine?

Love,
Bessie

————

San Francisco
September 13, 1915

Manly Dear,

I am perched on the side of Telegraph Hill watching the ships go by. There are twenty-six ships in sight and ten small sail boats. One of them is a hay boat. It looks like a load of hay floating on the water with three sails on it. There are about three thousand tons of hay on board, one thousand down below decks and the two thousand on deck. It looks strange to see a load of hay floating on the water. It has come down some river from the alfalfa farms. Just now a British trading ship is going past outward bound, perhaps to be sunk by a German submarine. It is the freight steamers, you know, that they particularly want to get. It has gone past now and I hear the blast of its whistle. I suppose it is meeting some other ship. Now in the immediate foreground is a white ferry steamer and farther over an orange-colored Exposition ferry bound for the Exposition grounds. There are two lumber ships going by loaded with lumber. One of them is coming in to the pier. It is loaded a little unevenly and tips some to one side. I suppose it lists to starboard or to larboard or something. One sailing ship with dirty-looking sails with clean new patches on them has sailed in and dropped anchor. The sails are running down. Now someone is getting over the side into a little boat. This ship looks like a tramp and I think it is. A ship is going by now that came from the Hawaiian Islands with a cargo of sugar. It is empty and riding high in the water. A Hawaiian passenger ship has passed bound for the Hawaiian Islands and Uncle Sam's gray battleship is lying anchored a little way out. Little white yachts are scurrying among the larger ships.

There are six piers in sight with all kinds of ships tied up to them. One is a British freighter with the flag flying, glad to be safe for awhile I suppose. Another is a Greek ship with several strings of flags flying in the wind. They say that is a sign that it will leave soon.

The hills across the bay look beautiful through the fog and Berkeley and Oakland show dimly. The tide is rising now and pouring in through the Golden Gate. I can see just how far it has come in by the white caps on the water. Goat Island is right in front. That is where the naval training school is.

One little sailing boat has just gone by, sailing so close into the wind* that the tip of the sail touches the water now and then. The man in sight is standing on the other edge of the boat, out on the very edge to keep it from tipping over. But I could watch these ships go by and write you about them all day. Rose is thinking of moving out here. There is a little house she can rent which faces all this. It is built on the side of the hill and there is a balcony overhanging the steep hillside. It looks

*Laura must have meant "so close-hauled."

over the roofs of the houses below, and the piers and all the beautiful bay is spread out like a picture. An artist friend of Rose's, a dear girl, is moving into another little house right next to the one Rose can get. The places are rather dilapidated but can be fixed very cosily.

I am glad Inky is more cheerful and that you are getting along all right. Rose and I are going to do some work on stories together this week.

Lovingly,
Bessie

I forgot to say that there is a wireless station on Goat Island. I can see the mast. From there they talk to Honolulu in the Hawaiian Islands. I saw a yacht race this afternoon too. Twenty-one little sail boats with their white sails filling out with the wind came into sight like a flock of white ducks. They sailed to a certain point, then turned and raced back out of sight behind the headland. It was very pretty.

Rolf Pelkie who has drawn pictures for the *Bulletin* has disappeared without a word of warning. The rumor among the newspaper people is that he was a German spy.*

―――――

San Francisco
September 13, 1915

Manly Dear,

About the horse—if it is the horse you want I suppose it would be a good plan to change a horse as old as Buck for a six-year-old. The $50 you would give to boot, you would just be giving for the colt and it would soon be the third horse for the farm, or would sell and buy the third horse. However, be sure the mare is the horse you want so you will not be out of a team.

What a shame to have the grapes stolen. Have you any idea who it was?

Honest fact, I'm homesick but there are so

―――――

*He wasn't. His absence is unexplained, but he returned to the city for a long and successful career. Rumors of spying and sabotage by the Kaiser's agents were on the rise in 1915, and some of them were borne out later. In fact, before his death Warren K. Billings wrote the Editor that he was inclined to believe that German agents had actually set off the bomb in the celebrated Mooney-Billings case of 1916 in a misguided effort to head off U.S. participation in the war. The truth remains unknown.

many interesting things still to be seen and I am here, that I feel I must see some more of them before I leave. Then I do want to do a little writing with Rose to get the hang of it a little better so I can write something that perhaps I can sell.

Don't buy the horse unless you are sure it is gentle. I do not want you hurt while I am gone or any other time for that matter. Could you get it on trial? What about getting a horse at a sale? If there has been so much washing away of crops, etc., perhaps there will be a good many sales—$125 is not a bargain, but full price unless the price of horses has advanced. But you are on the ground. Do whatever you think best.

I am going to do the things I absolutely must do before I come home. There are a few, you know, such as going over some of my copy with Rose and going out to the Fair a couple more times, and then I am coming home. Rose is very busy with her copy and the house and all, so we do not accomplish much in a day. I am doing what she will let me to help so she will have time to help me and to go play at the

Fair with me. I am anxious to get back and take charge of the hens again. Believe me, there is no place like the country to live and I have not heard of anything so far that would lead me to give up Rocky Ridge for any other place.

I want to go to Petaluma and see the chicken farm but that will cost something and I may not do that.

Anyhow, I'm sure that together we can figure out easier ways of doing the chicken work when you have a little time to fix things. I hope nothing happens there to make my trip overly expensive for it has done me lots of good and I think it has done Rose good too. Gee! It will be good to get busy again on my job.

Love to Inky & yourself,
Bessie

San Francisco
September 15, 1915

Manly Dear,
I am sending you the printed story of

[Rose's] something that Rose and I actually saw and heard on the Zone.

Yesterday Gillette and I went to the Presidio, the army reservation where the soldiers live in barracks and in tents. There are beautiful residences where the officers live and a wide cement drive where automobiles and carriages go, with dirt roads for the cavalry. We arrived by the guardhouse just in time to see them bring out the prisoners. They looked as though they had been having too hilarious a time! Gillette said they likely overstayed their leave and so were being punished.

All this soldier place is along the shore out where the disappearing guns guard the Golden Gate. They looked ugly, crouched in their hiding place behind the hills. We could see them but were not allowed to go close to them. Big signs said "Unauthorized persons will be detained by the sentinels." We saw at least fifty of these huge iron monsters, twelve- and sixteen-inch guns, and there were batteries hidden behind woods and one great encampment with batteries where we could not even go inside the wire enclosure to see any signs of the guns. There were smaller guns on wheels scattered around and an enormous searchlight on wheels. It was under cover but the great doors were open and men were working to make it even more spick and span than it already was. It was close beside the cement road which runs all the way around the edge of the cliffs, at the foot of which is the ocean.

Just across the narrow part where the passage is from the ocean to the gulf, were four forts on the other side, one of which is the highest fort in the world. We saw the stables where the cavalry horses and the mules are kept. Any number of horses and mules are tied on each side of a long rope stretched across the yards and immense barns. They all looked fat and well cared for. We met soldiers on foot, on horseback, and saw them at work at different things. Everyone seemed to be busy about their affairs and everything was so clean and well kept.

Gillette has a friend who is a lieutenant in the Navy and he has given Gillette his card with a note on the back saying to show him every courtesy. This will throw the battleship wide open to us, as he is next to the highest in rank on the ship. They will take special pains to show us and explain to us and we three are planning to go out tomorrow. This lieutenant holds the world's record for marksmanship with the big guns on a battleship and is in charge of the reserves at the naval training school on Goat Island.

I did not write you particularly of the time we spent at the Fair, for I saw so much that I could not describe it all. Rose and I are going out this afternoon. We are going to see the livestock exhibit and the "Dogs of All Nations." Then we are going on board a launch and sail out into the ocean to meet the sunset. Then we are coming back and stay on the Zone until they put us out, about eleven. The Zone is filled with a crowd of merrymakers and is full of music and lights and funny things. I am making notes in a book of the different things I see at the Exposition and when I come home I can describe them to you.

Rose has finished her story and has now to write another and have it all finished in nineteen days when they will begin to publish it.

Love,
Bessie

ENCLOSED NEWSPAPER CLIPPING

SAILORS AT SEA ON THE ZONE

They were five sailors, and they had come on shore for a good time.

You could see by their eager, determined expressions that they meant it to be a very good time indeed—a really memorable time that would color with happy recollections a long voyage at sea.

And they had hastened with eager feet to the Zone.

But the Zone is a bewildering place to be when one is looking for *a* good time—there are so many good times on every hand.

And the five sailors were obliged to choose ONE—at least, one to begin with.

Here were the barkers—"Watch him! Watch him! He's foxy! He's foxy!"

And the spielers—"This way! This way!

Carnival of music and mirth!"

And the ballyhoos—"Tum! Tum! Tum! Whoopee! Al-la-ah-hooOO! See the hula-hula-hula-hula!"

The five sailors hesitated, and dodged the Irish jaunting car. They hesitated again, and were accosted by the Waffle Clown. They moved down the street and conferred together.

"The Streets of Cairo suits me," said one.

"We've bloomin' well seen the real thing. I want to see something new—say we try the Educated Horse," said another.

"'E's tame. I vote we go to the Forty-Niners."

"I 'ear they sell nawthin' but soft drinks. Let's see the 'Uman Midgets."

And so they conferred, coming to no conclusion.

Until suddenly five pairs of roving eyes caught sight of the one irresistible attraction. For a moment they stood and gazed, and listened. Then, in single file, with beaming faces and not a dissenting murmur, they approached the ticket booth and purchased tickets, they mounted the sloping approach to the platform, passed the ticket-taker, and began a hilarious round of giddy joy.

The five sailors had finally found the one attraction on the Zone irresistible to them.

And they had paid their dimes at the "Old Red Mill" for a boat ride.

———

San Francisco
September 21, 1915

Manly Dear,

Yesterday I saw the "Dogs of All Nations" and was rather disappointed in them. There were some interesting ones, among them some of Perry's team who went to the North Pole. Then there was an Irish Wolf Hound, which breed the man in charge said was very rare. The one we saw was as large as a yearling steer and was only thirteen months old and thin. They said he was worth $3,000, perhaps like Mr. Quigley's thousand-dollar one, but this one was certainly a monster. It seemed impossible that it could be a dog and be so large.

We saw some fine Percheron horses and some Belgian horses and the dearest little Hungarian ponies. They are the size of

Shetlands. One was a dapple gray with silver mane and tail. He was beautiful. The man said he was worth $500. While he was having the pony play around on the end of the halter a man came by with a very large Belgian horse and they looked so funny as they passed by each other.

There were some lovely Kentucky race and riding horses, and believe me, they can all have their automobiles that want them. I would have me a Kentucky riding horse if I could afford it.

And OH I saw the Carnation milk cows being milked with a milking machine. And it milked them clean and the cows did not object in the least. The man in charge took your address and if you get any literature be sure and save it, for this machine is certainly a success and I can tell you about it when I come.

I have had a trip on the bay out into the sunset. It was wonderful and the more the boat rolled on the waves the better I liked it. I did not get dizzy at all. We went out to the highest fort in the world and around by the quarantine station on Angel Island and then back to the anchorage. The fog rolled up and came down on us and we could not see the land in any direction. The ocean swell came in through the Golden Gate and rocked the boat and we could imagine we were away out on the ocean. It was just a little steam yacht we were on and Rose and I stood up in the very front and let the spray and the mist beat into our faces and the wind blow our hair and clothes and the boat roll under our feet and it was simply glorious.

Since then we have taken the ferry boat and gone down the bay to Sausalito. We took a loaf of bread with us and threw it to the sea gulls and they followed us clear across the bay. We would throw a piece of bread out and they would try to catch it but it usually fell into the water and then they would drop down after it and squall and try to get it away from each other. I enjoyed the boat ride very much but it was not so good as the other because the boat was larger and would not pitch. We got off at Sausalito and stayed over two boats. We walked around the town, which is built all up and down the sides of the hills and the streets are crooked and no two houses built on the same level. It is a beautiful little place.

It was getting twilight when we took the boat back and we went out and up the path of the moon on the waves. We counted thirty-one ships and small motorboats anchored in the harbor as we came away. It was a beautiful sight, and we stood out on the deck as close as we could get to the water all the way home.

The lights at the Exposition made it look like fairyland and the lights of the city rising on the hills, row after row behind, linked it all with the stars until one could not tell where the lights stopped and the stars began. San Francisco is a beautiful, wonderful city and the people in it all seem so friendly—I mean the people one meets on the streets who are perfect strangers.

There seems to be a spirit of comradeship and informality among men and women alike. I thought it was because of the Fair but Rose says it is always that way. Perhaps it is because of the fire when they all got so well acquainted.

Sunday we went for a twelve-mile streetcar ride in all directions over the city and it only cost us a nickel apiece because of transfers.

We saw the old mission that was the first of San Francisco,* founded by the priest who put the stone cross on the hill for the ships at sea. This old mission church is decorated by the Indians of those early days. The rafters and beams of the ceiling are stained in Indian designs and the pictures and wall decorations are the work of the Indians also. Before the mission runs the "King's Road" which reached all up and down the coast.† It was traveled in those days by the priests as they went from one mission to another and of course by Indians and others. There were bells on all the highest points and there was a system of ringing the bells in such a way as to carry news from point to point so that it could travel all up and down the coast.

After we left the mission we went on out five miles to where they are starting a new suburb of the city. There is a beautiful view of the bay. Then we came back through Butcher Town and passed the China Basin and up

* Mission Dolores, nucleus of the city, originally the Mission of Saint Francis of Assisi.
† El Camino Real, the highway built by the Spanish colonists then ruled by Carlos III.

town again where we stopped at a moving picture show and saw Charlie Chaplin, who is horrid. I mean we saw him act in the pictures.

I am tired and must go to bed early so I can go to San Jose tomorrow. Besides I must leave something to tell you when I come home or you will not be glad to have me.

Lovingly,
Bessie

The foghorn on Alcatraz is crying out at regular intervals so it must be that the fog is getting thick. Every few minutes I hear the bellow of a steamer's whistle as it comes in or meets or passes another boat. The foghorn on Alcatraz is the most lonesome sound I ever heard and I don't see how the prisoners on the island stand it.

San Francisco
September 21, 1915

Manly Dear,

Rose is running around town getting the material together for another story and I have just come back from seeing the Germans capture Przemyś in a moving picture theater. The pictures are true, being actually taken on the ground. It is horrible because it looks so implacable, so absolutely without mercy. I saw the big siege guns in action and saw them rock on their bases when they were fired. The Germans dropped 700,000 shells on the Russian position in four hours. They fired from the four sides. It is no wonder the men can not stand and face such shells especially as they (the guns) are always so far out of reach. These were ten miles away.

Tomorrow Rose and I are going to see the Santa Clara Valley and San Jose. This is one valley where they have the sea breeze and Rose thinks we might like to live there.* I would not think of living in an interior valley. It is a worse heat than Florida and it is all the year around. I saw and felt it as I came, you know. I asked Rose and she said she would not live herself where she could not get the sea breezes.

The first of next week we are going to Mill Valley, which is up the bay and the breezes

* Apparently Rose had been trying to persuade her mother to consider moving to California with Almanzo.

come. Land can be had there for two to three hundred an acre. The place is really a suburb of San Francisco and San Francisco would be our market. There are a few miles by rail and then across the bay on the ferry. Rose and Gillette both say that we could make our living on an acre raising eggs for the San Francisco market and have the most of what we could get for the [Mansfield] farm out at interest. Eggs are now forty-five cents and the farmer is getting forty-two, but I have not yet been able to find out what the poultry men have to pay for the feed. Rose says we will ask some of them when we go to the place. The big poultry raising place of California is just fifteen miles from Mill Valley. It is called Petaluma. They also say that I could write here as well or better than I can there, but that, you know, is very uncertain. Anyhow, I am going to see it and find out all I can about it and the Santa Clara Valley, then I can tell you when I come home and we can decide whether we will look into it any more.

Rose is planning to buy a lot in Mill Valley and build a little place to live and so stop rent. She says she can pay [what she now pays in] rent toward the place and have the place left, while now she pays the money out and has nothing to show for it.

Gillette has no regular job but gets extra work whenever he can, and has some good prospects for work, but just now Rose is carrying them both. She is getting $30 a week but the house rent and the bills take it nearly all. It costs every time one turns around. Even the car-fare counts up for they have to go all over town about their work and the distances are too great to walk. Rose had to give up moving to Telegraph Hill. We found out that the landlady, who lives next door with seven children, gets drunk and fights. Not a good neighborhood, you see, and that is why the rent was lower.

I got to San Francisco with $15 left. I have not spent any of it since I got here and Rose gave me $10 yesterday to give to you when I get home. She gave it to me for keeping and said she thought she could spare it. Of course if anything should go wrong to make expenses more, or there should be any change in her job before I leave, she might have to have it back, but she thinks not and says she intends to do as she said and make up to you for what you are losing by my being away.

If Gillette lands a regular job as he expects, he says he will lift the $500 [mortgage] that is on the [Mansfield] place but I think we must not count on that for of course anything is uncertain until it is landed. However, if Rose does make out to give us something for my time and things go right, perhaps we can pay a hundred on the $200 note, and then if the hens will help us worry that out this winter then the $250 which Gillette has secured to us on his commissions will half pay the note on the farm.* I am being as careful as I can and I am not for a minute losing sight of the difficulties at home or what I came for. Rose and I are blocking out a story of the Ozarks for me to finish when I get home. If I can only make it sell, it ought to help a lot and besides, I am learning so that I can write others for the magazines. If I can only get started at that, it will sell for a good deal more than farm stuff. We are slow about it, for Rose has to do the work that draws her pay. I do the housework

* It seems likely that Rose and Gillette had borrowed $250 from Laura and Manly to get started.

so that she will have time to help me with my learning to write and to go with me to see the things that I must see before I go away.

I do enjoy being with Rose but I am so homesick it hurts. Rose has worked so hard to save the money to get me out for the visit that it seems a shame to leave before my ticket expires, but I am going to try and get things done so that I can come home the middle of October, which will be about three weeks yet if I have it right. I will not be able to see Thirkield's brother. Sacramento is too long a railroad trip to take just for that. I came through there when I came here but am going back another way.

Mrs. Cobb is away off my line of travel coming home. I would like to see her very much but I do not feel that I can pay what it would cost. Places are so far apart out here—people do not realize. These mountains are like walls and on the train one climbs and climbs and then comes almost back to where he was before.

Rose wants very much to save enough so that she can go with me and start me home by way of Los Angeles. To do that I will have to lose this end of my ticket and it will cost my fare and hers down and hers back. That is if we do as we want and go by steamer. It is my only chance to have a trip on the ocean. Any other will cost too much. I am rather afraid I will have to give that up but if I do manage to go that way I will see Mrs. Comstock and West if I can find him. I know it must be hard for you and I feel guilty to have come, but I'll help you all I can when I get back and try to tell you all I have seen and you will not have to cook any more.

Mrs. Cooley must have been a sight, and if you don't mind I would rather not dress that way.

I like to get your letters but of course I do not expect you to write when you have so much to do. Just a card or a word now and then so I will know you are all right. I have not had a word from De Smet and I have written them twice. Once when I first got here, and then again telling them I had heard from you and asking how Ma was.*

Be good to Inky and yourself and take care of things the best you can. I do hope nothing

* Laura's father had died, but her mother was living in De Smet with Mary, Laura's blind sister.

will go very wrong until I get back and not then of course. I hope Mr. Nall came back. I hate to think of you alone.

Your loving Bessie

———

POSTCARD

September 22, 1915
(Picture of Ridgway's Tea Exhibit, Food Products Building)

Dear Papa—Showed Bessie the dogs and cows and horses. Saw a milking machine. We are sending literature about it. Save it. This week we are going down into the Santa Clara Valley and show Bessie California orchards. Wish you were here. Tell Inky not to be jealous. We did not see any dogs we liked better than him.

Rose

———

San Francisco
September 23, 1915

Dear Manly,

I am very tired this morning after my trip seeing the Santa Clara Valley yesterday. I started at 8:30 in the morning, rode for half an hour on the streetcar and then one and one half hours on the train. This brought us to San Jose. Rose showed me around the city for awhile. I like the town very much. We had lunch at a restaurant and then took a jitney bus for Los Gatos. From there we went to Palo Alto by electric streetcar and there took the train back to San Francisco, getting home about seven o'clock in the evening. I enjoyed the day but am glad I am not going anywhere today.

The trip took us clear around the valley so that I saw all parts of it. It is a beautiful place to look at if one likes to see very intensive orchard raising and handling. The bottom of the valley is as level as a floor and the foothills rising to mountains completely surround it except for the side open to the bay and the ocean breezes. It was very, very hot in the sun but cool in the shade and with a cool breeze blowing. Most of the valley is in orchard and the trees are of course set with mathematical precision, all trimmed to exactly the same shape and form, all the same size and the ground beneath them all as smooth and bare as a very flat smooth garden spot. The trees are trimmed in the shape of an inverted cone and are trimmed back so that they do not grow tall. They make no shade that one could stand in to rest a moment. The orchards are all irrigated of course. Ditches are plowed through the orchards in the spring and the water is run through them every six weeks through the bearing season. Then after that the ground is plowed smooth and is left that way for awhile. They are just now beginning to plow the ditches and let the water in again for the fall irrigation. It looked ugly to me, someway, to see the men working in the hot sun letting the water into the ditches so it would run around the feet of the tree while the tree itself and all its leaves were loaded with dust from the plowing. They did look as though they wanted a drink so much.

I saw some dairy farms which looked about as they might anywhere except that they too were dry and dusty. There were some chicken ranches, but the hens here are all kept in runs that are perfectly bare ground. The green stuff is cut and fed them and to me they looked dusty, hot and unhappy, though I suppose they were well cared for and comfortable.

The farm houses are fine and the places look prosperous. The roads are splendid and the little towns are lovely. The mountains which can be seen in the distance or close up, according as to where one is, are very beautiful, with the changing fog around them. However, I would not like to live there for I do not enjoy the heat and the dust, and the flat, flat land is tiresome to look at. You would like that to work, of course, but we could not get any good land for less than $500 an acre and from all I can find out I do not believe it would be the best thing to do even if one had money enough. [The threat of] prohibition is ruining the grape industry of California and it is only a question of a little time when the grape grower will go out of the business except, of course, those who furnish fresh grapes for eating. Five hundred dollars an acre is too much to pay for land to farm on, even in California. If we had the thousand dollars I would rather put it at interest than buy two acres of land to work hard on. Wouldn't you?

I am going to see the land around Mill Valley and find out all I can about it. Then if I come home by way of Los Angeles I will see about the country there, and at Pasadena, but I truly believe that when I come home and talk it all over with you we will decide to be satisfied where we are and figure out some way to cut down our work and retire right there. Gillette is trying to make me see how we could come out here and do scientific farming on a couple of acres at a great deal more profit, but we would have it all to learn and we are rather old dogs to learn new tricks, especially as we do not have to do so. The more I see here the more I think that I will come home and put all my attention on the chickens.

I am getting some pointers on how to handle more of them for of course there will need to be more in order to get much from it, but if I can make $1 a year on a hen there, why be to all the trouble to move out here and learn new conditions when that is about all they make here? And if I would have to keep 1500 chickens or more to make a success here I do not see why I can not handle as many there, and all without the trouble of moving.

We can either make you comfortable in spite of the cold in some way or let you go south to spend the coldest weather.

Oh, I hope you are fairly comfortable and can get help to take care of the crop so we will have the chicken feed for this year. It is fine that the stuff grew so well. Feed the hens some linseed meal so they will grow their feathers before cold weather. The laying ration, you know, is four parts of bran, two of corn chop, one of bone and one half of oil meal. I suppose you are giving them all the bone they want as we always do, and I believe I would increase the oil meal to get them to grow their feathers. If there are any sunflower seeds give them to the hens now. That helps with the feathers too.

Gillette and Rose will get their deferred commissions soon or find out that the men can not make their payments, in which case they will lose them. I think if I am on the ground when Gillette gets his I can get the $250 he owes us. If I am not here to strike when the iron is at the right heat I do not know whether we will get any more than the $250 or not. He will have enough if he gets it so that he can lend it to us and he says he will, but money runs through his fingers like water and he might not get around to send it to me until it was all gone.

I have the battleship yet to see and Mill Valley and then I am through with sight-seeing. Oh, of course there are things here that I would love to see, enough to last a year, but I will have seen all I am very particular about. I want to finish blocking out my story but I will likely have that done by the time the sight-seeing is over and then I will break away and come home.

Rose has a very hard assignment from the paper now and it is keeping her busy at work. She was sent on our trip yesterday and I just went along. Today she is at the office while I am resting.

Gillette has worked for the last few days covering a couple of conventions for a press syndicate. Just a short job. He has not yet managed to get on permanently anywhere. It is my private opinion that the State of California is seeing hard times even though they will not admit it. I am sure that business is dull in a good many ways, from the talks we had with the real estate man yesterday and other straws.

Lovingly,
Bessie

————

POSTCARD

San Francisco
September 24, 1915

(Foothills near San Jose, Calif.)

Dear Manly,

    This is some of the country I saw on trip to San Jose, only the orchards are not in bloom now. Address my letters 1019 B. Vallejo St., San Francisco.

Bessie

————

San Francisco
September 28, 1915

Manly Dear,

    I did not get Wilhelm's letter so I suppose I missed one of yours too. I think they are rather careless with the mail at the office and so you had better send the letters to the house. Address them until further notice to 1019 B. Vallejo St., San Francisco.

Sunday afternoon I went over to Berkeley on the ferry steamer, about seven miles across the bay. We had a little lunch with us and ate it up on the top of one of the Berkeley hills. It is lovely crossing the bay. I always get at the front of the boat and on the lower deck to be as near the water as possible. Then I stand and hold to the rope and let the boat lift and sway under my feet and the spray and wind beat in my face and watch the gulls. After we cross the bay we take an electric train which is out on the end of the long pier.

I must tell you about these piers reaching out into the bay. The water is shallow on that side and they are dredging from the bottom of the bay and taking the rock and dirt to build out the shore. It is made land for one mile out now where these piers run and they are filling in between the piers. There are several of the piers. Oh, I don't know how many, a dozen I should guess. The cities of Oakland and Berkeley are doing the work and they have appropriated $10,000,000 to build land out as far as Goat Island, which is about another mile, making two miles in all of made land. They are doing this to save five minutes in time from Oakland and Berkeley to San Francisco. Oakland is once and a half again as large as Kansas City, and Berkeley is about as large as Oakland, but they are really suburbs of San Francisco and if it were not for the bay they would be all one city. People live in Oakland and Berkeley and come every morning to their down town places of business in the city (San Francisco) and it is to save the five minutes on each trip every day for these people that the $10,000,000 is to be spent.

Berkeley is the "city of homes" and is a beautiful place both in its natural scenery and its buildings. Street after street of handsome residences, not apartment houses, lovely parks and the University of California with its numbers of buildings and wide beautiful drives and walks. I went all around and through them and then to see the "Greek Theater." This is an outdoor theater, built on the hillside which forms a natural amphitheater. It is built exactly like an old Greek theater and is the only copy of it in existence today. The stage and dressing rooms are a stone building at the foot of the hills, or rather the dressing rooms are the building and the stage is a cement platform with no roof. There are large stone columns in the front of the dressing rooms, dividing the opening on the stage. The center circle before the stage is a sawdust ring for wrestling matches, etc., and the seats rise one above the other like a grandstand only in a semicircle up the sides of the hills, which completely surround them and rise above the highest seat like a rampart, completely around the seats, with tall pine trees growing on the top. There is no roof but the blue sky and the whole thing is very wonderful and beautiful besides being world famous.

We climbed the hill behind the Greek Theater and ate our lunch with Oakland, Berkeley, the blue bay and the city of San Francisco spread at our feet, with still more hills or mountains rising at our backs and a blue, blue sky above us. And this was beautiful Berkeley, "the city of homes."

After lunch we wandered down among the paths of the University grounds and so to the car line which we took to Oakland, and so home across the bay from another pier and on another steamer. From Berkeley to Oakland, you know, is following around the shore of the bay, although we were out of sight of it because of the houses. There is no space between the two—they are really one city and it is impossible to tell where the one ends and the other begins. It is wonderful to cross the bay at night out at the front of the boat near the water and I would never get tired of seeing the lights of San Francisco as the boat comes in. The ferry tower is very tall and all a mass of electric lights, and across it are the words in electric lights, "San Francisco invites the World—Panama-Pacific Exposition 1915," and then there are all the other electric lights and signs. I am getting so I can find my way around a little and even cross Market Street among the jitneys without being frightened.

Rose gave a little tea party for me yesterday, just a few of the girls and women who work on the *Bulletin* and who write. If you should see on the Margin of Life page a series of little stories, "The People in Our Apartment House," you may read them knowing that they are *true*. Rose is writing them and the "little artist girl who lives in the basement"* makes the pictures. I like Rose's women friends very much. The men at the *Bulletin* office are only acquaintances. Some of them are very pleasant to meet and some I dislike very much. Did I tell you that the Pelkie who was doing the artist work on the paper when I was at home has disappeared and there is a suspicion around the office that he was in some way connected with the German spy system here?

Yesterday after the 4 P.M. tea party we went down to the ferry to see Gillette's brother Edson start home. He came out unexpectedly and was in the city only one day on business so all we saw of him was a little while at the ferry station.

I love a ride on the streetcars at night and to get to the ferry station we go through the famous Barbary Coast. Most of the buildings on the street are closed and dark now, but a little nearer the station is what they call the "waterfront," where every building on the

* Later to become the renowned Berta Hader, author-illustrator (with her husband) of children's books.

street is a saloon. Gillette says the sailors come ashore there with all their pay from a six-months' voyage and they have to have some place to get rid of their money. He says that if they have not managed to spend it all by two or three o'clock in the morning someone will obligingly hit them over the head with a piece of gaspipe and take it away from them.

I am glad Mr. Nall came back and that you are going to cement the rats and mice out. What an awful lot of rain you are having. I should think it would make the fall feed good. Here every morning the fog is so thick it looks as though it would rain, but towards noon it clears away and the sun shines usually until towards night when the fog drifts in again from the ocean like smoke and everything is dull and gray again. Rose is very busy writing her story and I keep busy doing one thing and another. She expects to get it all written this week and then she will likely be able to have a few days to play and we will see Mill Valley and the battleship and have another day at the Fair. Of course I am enjoying the visit but I want to see you and Inky.

Bessie

———

POSTCARD

September 29, 1915

(Exhibit Palace, Carnation Milk Condensery, Pacific International Exposition, San Francisco 1915)

Dear Manly,

I'll tell you all how they condense milk when I come. Was shown all over this very particularly.

Bessie

———

San Francisco
September 29, 1915

Manly Dear,

I spent yesterday afternoon at the Exposition. Rose went out to see an engineer at the Southern Pacific exhibit to get some facts for her railroad story and as Gillette had the day off we both went along and wandered around while she was talking to him.

We saw the kangaroos and the wallabies at the Australian exhibit. One kangaroo was taking his afternoon nap in a bed he had scooped out in the sand. The sun was shining brightly and very hot on his bed in the center of the wire yard and he lay flat on his back with his legs all sticking straight up and slept. A lady kangaroo was making herself a bed in the sand and another one was eating mud. A wallaby was hopping around. It looks like the kangaroos, only smaller, and its fur was gray instead of yellowish-brown. The kangaroos looked just like pictures of them, only more so. Their front parts are so much smaller and out of proportion to their hind parts that they look ugly and they seem very awkward as they hop around.

The Australian exhibit was mostly wool and minerals. The New Zealand Building was near. Their exhibit was wood and woolen goods and moving pictures showing harvesting scenes, fishing scenes, surf bathing, loading of ships with oysters, hemp, wool, and cheeses for export. There was also a stock show showing their cattle and horses, in pictures I mean, and they were fine. Do you remember when we talked of going to New Zealand? I liked the pictures of the country very much.

We went through the France and Belgium Building but our time was limited. Rose and I are going through them again and I will write about them then. They are wonderful.

We met Rose in the Hawaiian Gardens in the Horticultural Building. They are a delightful combination of flowers and shrubs, and a large pavilion where Hawaiian coffee and pineapple juice and salad and other combinations of pineapple are served at little tables. There is a fountain in the center and water vines and shrubs and flowers around the fountain's rim. The fountain and a little space are enclosed with golden ropes and there are marble pedestals inside with canaries in cages on them. At one side is a balcony where a Hawaiian band plays and sings their native songs, which are lovely. The canaries have heard the music so long that at certain places they take up the tune and sing an accompaniment. It is beautiful. The waiters are Hawaiian men and girls and it's a delightful place to sit and rest, listen to the music and sip either coffee or delicious pineapple juice. In the gardens are all kinds of strange plants and flowers and gold fishes in rock tanks. There are the immense tree ferns, ferns with stems as large as the trunks of trees and growing as high, date palms and other curious things.

We went from here to the Food Products Building where everything eatable is made and sold. Too long for a letter. I'll have to tell you about it.*

Then we went to the Manufacturers' Building and there I saw something I'm sure will interest you. It was the "Keen Kutter" exhibit. In the center of the space, which was nearly two hundred feet square, was a river and a waterfall. The waves were chains, the waterfall was chains on a windlass, and the broken water below the falls was chains. Everything about the exhibit was worked by electricity. The waves were rolling down and over the waterfall. The broken water was running away below and a ship, the steel hull of which was a huge knife, sailed across the river above the falls, and a great snake made of some shining cutlery stuff crawls across at the

* What she told Manly must have been similar to the article she wrote for the Missouri *Ruralist* that appears in the Appendix.

foot of the picture. Above this scene is an arch made of glistening spoons of different sizes. At the upper right-hand corner was a gigantic pocket knife with four blades that kept opening and shutting and at the upper left-hand corner was a row of seven blacksmiths standing each at his anvil with a different tool in his hand. At stated times first one and then another would beat the tool on the anvil with his hammer, sharpening it apparently. At the center top were two windmills made of ax blades continually turning. At each side of the center (the center was the waterfall) was a fountain with the long streams of spray made of wire and the water made of bits, such as you use with your brace. The upper part of the water was just medium-size bits and then there was a rim on the fountain and then a circle of larger bits. They were all turning in the direction of boring, so it looked as though they were water running down, striking the rim, and then running down again. The illusion was *good*. The name "Keen Kutter Cutlery" was written above the whole thing with shiny padlocks and the whole thing was in motion moved by electricity. It was very interesting and it was positively uncanny to see that huge pocket knife open and shut, open and shut, as though it were alive and moving itself.

To cap the day, as we came home on the streetcar a man sat near us who was chewing gum. He wore a stiff hat pulled down tight on his head and every time he chewed, his hat moved up and down fully two inches, up and down, up and down, with perfect regularity as though he were worked by electricity.

Regards to Mr. Nall.

Lovingly,
Bessie

———

San Francisco
October 1, 1915

Manly Dear,

Rose gave me a ten-dollar gold piece last night. This makes $20 she has given me and makes $30 in gold I have to bring home with me. I have $5 in change which I expect I will have to spend to get me home—sleeping car berth, food, etc. I mentioned going home to Rose and she begged very hard for me to stay as long as my ticket will let me, which will be November 15. She said she would keep on making it up to me for my time if I would only stay. You see, she has given me $5 a week for the time I have been here.

I am wondering if I would not earn more toward paying off the debts if I stayed in that way, and if you could get the fall work done and things in shape for winter if I did. How about it? If I stay the month of October, you see, I would have $60 to bring home with me if nothing happens to Rose's job, and that would help a lot. But of course it would not pay to do it if it will make you lose the potato crop or the other crops or anything like that. You are the one to say, because it is you who are having the hard time and you know how things are there.

Gillette just missed getting a good job this week by about an hour. He is gone today to see if he can do anything on a real estate deal. If it works he will make $150 or $200. If not, he has lost his expenses. There are a good many newspaper men here out of jobs. Gillette thinks that it is perhaps because there are so many out here for the year to see the Fair. He says if he can get a little ahead, a couple of hundred dollars, he believes he will try for a job in St. Louis or Kansas City. Rose says she would like to work in St. Louis and be where she could run down home, but she has such a good job here that she can not afford to give it up until she has a little ahead or a good job for sure back there. She is putting a part of her salary in the savings bank every week, besides running the house and what she gives me and Gillette's expense while he is trying to get something. He gets extra work every once in awhile and when he draws his pay he turns it all over to Rose and then every day takes just enough for his streetcar fare, lunch down town, and cigars.

Lovingly,
Bessie

———

POSTCARD

October 4, 1915

(Carnation Stock Farm. One of the dairy farms which supplied fresh milk to condenseries to be evaporated, sterilized and hermetically sealed as Carnation Milk.)

Went to a "movie" theater last night that cost $600,000. Seats 4,000 people. Largest in U.S.

Lovingly, Bessie

———

San Francisco
October 4, 1915

Manly Dear,

I came home from down town by myself today. Rose's boss, managing editor, called her to come down to the office at twelve. She works at home, you know, and has been working very hard on a railroad story which was to begin in the Thursday paper. She has it nearly finished. I went down with her to see what was wanted and she thought that likely he wanted some little change made in the story.

What he wanted was that she should interview an Austrian musician who is giving concerts here. He is an international figure and a very wonderful player of the violin. He served four weeks in the Austrian army against the Russians and is wounded so that they will not have him any more. He has made some statements to the papers to the effect that there will be nothing worthwhile left in Europe when the war is over unless something is done to save a little from the wreck.

The money he gets for his playing is to be used for the artists in Europe (of whatever nationality) who need help to keep them alive. He says they are dying of starvation after they come out of the army as he has. He and his wife have adopted forty-three soldiers' orphans and are going to feed, clothe, and educate them as though they were truly their own.

Well, Rose's boss told her to go see him and get a story of his life and have it ready to start Thursday in place of the one she has been writing. They will publish the one she has been at work on later. This means that she will have to write it in a hurry, just ahead of the press.

So she went to interview the man and I came home.

There is a house part way down the hill where we live, the materials for which were brought around the Horn in the old days. The man who built it and his wife lived there until they were old and then they quarreled and the man deeded the wife half the house and lot, and had the house cut straight down through the middle and moved his half over onto his half of the lot and they lived there until they died. The house is up on the hill from the street.

A high rock wall runs along the street and in it is an iron gate. When one goes in the gate, he goes up four stone steps then turns and goes up a flight of stone steps. These steps are all inside the stone wall. Solid stone is on each side and overhead. At the top of these stone stairs one comes out into the outdoors on a stone walk. From here one can go around the head of the stairs on a little stone balustrade and out on a little stone balcony overhanging the street, or turn the other way, go up some broad deep stone steps for a little way, then up some more stone stairs and then some wooden stairs to the front door of the house. From the front room of the house there is a view over the tops of the houses and out on the bay. The little artist girl [Berta] who illustrated some of my verses has rented the front part of the house and is moving in. I love to go there just for the sake of going up those stone stairs inside the stone wall.

There was a little earthquake shock here Saturday night, or at least the paper said so the next morning. I did not feel it. It reached all up and down the coast and was heaviest in Nevada.

You surely must have got my letter by this time in which I told you about going out on the boat to see the sunset, but it will bear telling again. It was a small white launch and it cost fifty cents each. We were gone an hour. It started from the anchorage inside the fairgrounds and headed straight out for the Golden Gate where the sun was going down. Rose and I stayed on deck and right in the very front of the boat, where we saw only the rail and the few feet of deck in front of us and the rest was water. We kept one hand on a rope to steady ourselves and stood our feet a little wide apart and there we stood and faced the wind and the sun and the fog streaming in and felt the sway and pitch of the boat under our feet. Oh, it was delightful when we met the ocean swell near the Gate.

We went past the Exposition grounds and then the Presidio headlands to the Golden Gate and reached there just as the sun dipped out of sight. Then we turned and came around to come back on the other side of the bay, past the highest fort in the world and we knew that the huge disappearing guns were lurking there, past the buildings of the fort around the base of the mountain and the lighthouse out on the point of rock, past Angel Island where the quarantine station is, and then headed back across the bay for the anchorage. The fog closed in around us so that we were out of sight of land, sailing over a gray sea with the gray fog walling us in. The wind was driving the spray and fog in my face and the boat would rise and swoop and fall under my feet and it was glorious. Going on a ferry boat is not nearly so much fun, for the boat is so much larger that it rides steadier.

I am so glad Mr. Nall is with you and that you are getting the corn and peas taken care of, and so much of the other work done. Give my regards to Mr. Nall.

Lovingly,
Bessie

———

PRIVATE:*

Gillette has a job on the *Call* for a week now, so he will feel better. I tell you, this being in a city and out of a job is no fun.

Rose has syndicated† her Charlie Chaplin story. The syndicate is to take all the expense and trouble of selling to papers and magazines and Rose gets half the selling price. They tell her that they think they can sell it to papers in small towns and get an income from it of $500 a week for five weeks. The story runs for five weeks, you know, and the papers pay for it as they use it, at so much a week. Rose thinks that they are seeing things larger than they will turn out but she hopes to get something from it.

The more I see of how Rose works the

* In the original this is a separate piece of paper. Laura probably expected that Almanzo would read many of her letters aloud to friends in Mansfield, and she wanted to make sure this was not read.
† A syndicator offered a story written for a single newspaper to hundreds of papers all over the country for republication at a relatively small price to each.

better satisfied I am to raise chickens. I intend to try to do some writing that will count, but I would not be driven by the work as she is for anything and I do not see how she can stand it.

Lovingly,
Bessie

———

San Francisco
October 6, 1915

Manly Dear,

My last letter, you remember, was written when I had come home from down town by myself. Well, the funniest thing happened. When I came home, before I wrote you, I ran down to see the little artist girl. I was afraid Rose might come home while I was gone and be worried if I was not here, so I left a note for her saying where I was. When I came home from Berta's I carelessly left the note on the table and went on into my bedroom and wrote my letter to you on the typewriter. Well, Rose was worried about my coming home by myself, so when it was time that I should have arrived she phoned to me from down town.

Being at Berta's I, of course, did not answer, and they [the telephone operators] reported that they could not get me.

She finished her interview with Fritz Kreisler and went back to finish her business at the *Bulletin* office and as soon as she got there phoned again. Still no answer. She was worried, but had to go see the City Editor, and while she was in his office one of the girls in Miss Beatty's office kept trying to get me. Rose came down and the girl told her she could not get me, and Rose was terror-stricken and came rushing home as fast as the streetcar could bring her. All the way she kept thinking that an automobile had killed me—and remembering that I had nothing with me that would identify me, for I had not taken my purse. She rushed through the door thinking that she would phone the emergency hospital, and there on the table was my note saying I had gone to Berta's. She did not stop long enough to hear the typewriter clicking in the bedroom but rushed out again and down to Berta's. Berta said I had been gone for three quarters of an hour, so she ran to Bessie Beatty's across the street. I was not there.

Then Rose hurried to the little grocery where she buys her things, which was quite a little way, but I had not been there, so she rushed home again and while crossing the room to telephone the police she heard the typewriter and found me peacefully writing my letter to you.

I told her she should have thought I would find my way home somehow, but she was afraid I had been in an accident. She says that every day someone, and more usually more are run over by the automobiles, and said she would never let me out of her sight again. But nevertheless I went down town and back again by myself yesterday and I had to cross Market Street to get to the *Bulletin* office, and that is the worst street in the city. I had no trouble.

We have had the thickest fog ever for several days. All night and all day we can hear the sirens on the different islands and headlands, and the ferries and ships at anchor in the bay keep their foghorns bellowing. We can not see the bay at all nor any part of San Francisco except the few close houses on Russian Hill. The foghorns sound so mournful and distressed, like lost souls calling to each other through the void. (Of course, no one ever heard a lost soul calling, but that's the way it sounds.) It looks as though Russian Hill were afloat in a gray sea and Rose and I have taken the fancy that it is loosened from the rest of the land and floating across the sea to Japan. That is the feeling it gives one.

There are eight big ocean-going ships outside the Golden Gate that can not find their way in through the fog and are waiting for it to clear. One is a passenger ship from the Orient, one is a U.S. transport, one is a Greek tramp. The rest are passenger ships from the coast cities and one of them is filled with passengers and crew from a wrecked and abandoned ship. There they all are, so close to land and can't get in.

I must tell you about Rose's interview with Fritz Kreisler, the Austrian violinist who served four weeks in the trenches and came out wounded so that he is unfit for further service. I think I wrote you that he was sending all he could make back to help, not to carry on the war, but to save other artists from starving and to care for those forty-three children they have adopted.

He said there was no hatred for each other among the soldiers and that all these stories of barbarities committed by the soldiers of one side on the wounded of the other side were simply made up by the papers and those higher up for the sake of inflaming popular passion and creating a hatred. He said that both German and Russian, when gathering up the wounded from a battlefield, took them all, German and Russian, and treated them alike.

Among the children they are supporting are three Russian families. Mrs. Kreisler was a nurse with the Austrian army. He says she was so tenderhearted that when a wounded soldier could not die in peace for worrying about his children she would promise him that if Mr. Kreisler lived to come back they would take care of them. When he came back she had promised forty-three, among them were the three Russian soldiers.

He said that in one battle where the Austrians retreated the Russians gathered up among the wounded an Austrian with a shattered jaw. They fixed his wound as well as possible but he could not eat solid food. In the company were a few eggs and they fed them all to this wounded Austrian and went without themselves, not knowing how soon they would need them. Mr. Kreisler came to know about it because a few days later the Austrians charged and recaptured the place, and the wounded Austrian told them. This too when the Russians did not have enough of anything to eat. Remember that it is an Austrian telling this story of the Russians. Rose says both Fritz Kreisler and his wife are the loveliest people she has ever met.

We are going to the Greek Theater tomorrow to hear him play.

Eggs are fifty cents a dozen here now.

Take good care of yourself and Inky. I am anxious to get an answer to my letter in which I asked you to say how long I might stay. If I stay until my ticket expires which will be November 15, Rose will be able to take the ocean trip with me to Los Angeles. If I do not stay until that time I will have to give up seeing Los Angeles and the ocean trip and come home as my ticket reads.

Lovingly,
Bessie

———

San Francisco
October 14, 1915

Manly Dear,

It has been several days since I wrote you so I will begin back where I left off.

Rose and I went over to Berkeley to hear Fritz Kreisler, the Austrian, play the violin. This you know meant a trip across the bay, which is always such a pleasure, then a street-car ride through Oakland, for this time we landed at the Oakland pier, then a walk across the campus or college grounds to the Greek Theater which I have described to you before.

It was wonderfully beautiful at night. The lights were lit until the people were seated and when the concert began they were all turned off except the lights on the stage. The stage and the walls behind, like the wings of a theater, are white marble and the tops of the tall pines and eucalyptus trees showed above it. The hills rise around the amphitheater so that the seats as they rise one above the other have the solid hillside behind them. The hills rise still higher than the seats with the large trees growing on them, so as we sat in the theater the trees rose all around above us. The moon shone just above the stage and it was all so beautiful that when Kreisler's violin began to sing it made one's throat ache. There was a complete orchestra of stringed instruments to play the accompaniments to Kreisler. The music was the most beautiful I have ever heard. We sat for two hours, almost without breathing, listening to it. The seats were crowded and all we could see of the people was a dark blur and all the white faces. They were all as still and listening as intently as we were.

Then there was the ride home across the bay and by streetcar. We got home at one o'clock and were very tired. But, oh, the next day we were so stiff from sitting on those cold, hard rock seats for so long that we could hardly move. My tiredness settled in my eyes and I haven't been able to use them much since. Did I tell you I got a pair of as-good-as-gold-trimmed just plain magnifying glasses at the ten-cent store here? They help so much. I could not read or write without them but my eyes get so tired even when I use them that I'm afraid the man in Springfield was right and they need particular ones.

Oh, the other day as Rose and I walked down town we saw in the window of an antique shop a silver watch that weighs three pounds. It was made for a prospector from the very first silver ever mined in California. It was made in 1848. Beside it was a tray of small, beautiful, beautiful jeweled watches made in the 16th century (400 years ago) in France.

Sunday about five o'clock Rose finished writing for the day and she and I took a street-car for the ocean beach. We got off at Land's End and walked around by the shore to the Cliff House. We watched the waters awhile from the Cliff House balcony and then went down to the edge of the water on the shore where the waves could roll in at our feet and watched the beautiful colors of sunset fade away from sea and sky and the dark come over the waters. I do love the ocean so much—the sight of it and the sound of it and the smell of it.

Tuesday Rose and I spent all day at the

Fair. She let me plan the day as I wished, so we went down early—got to the grounds about 9:30.

First we looked at the kangaroos and wallabies. They are in a wire yard between the Australian and New Zealand Buildings. From there we went through the Australian Building and found there the most wonderful exhibit of native woods we have seen yet. I did not know that such beautiful woods grew anywhere and I did so wish you and Mr. Nall could see them.* They show each kind of wood in the rough, in slabs and timbers and planks. Then they have each kind finished and polished naturally, and then they have furniture made of each kind. Myrtle wood was the loveliest. There was a bedroom set of it. Price $2,000.00. Then there are different kinds of oak, among them the "silky oak" that looks just like watered silk. There are

---

* Almanzo was an accomplished cabinetmaker and carpenter. A number of his creations are on display today at the Wilder home in Mansfield, which is now the Laura Ingalls Wilder–Rose Wilder Lane Museum. Laura knew he would be interested in wood varieties as well as woodworking tools.

different kinds of pine and ever so many others. The hard woods of Australia are almost fireproof, and there are on exhibition some timbers that have been under water for thirty years, still sound. There were all kinds of grains and strange fruits and vegetables and mountains of wool and metals and minerals. We met a couple of Australian newspaper men, "press men," as they call them, and they told us a good deal about Australia and gave us a lot of literature which I will bring home. One of them was *Captain* somebody. He wore a fierce little mustache, waxed and twisted so tight that it stood straight out and he had the scar of an old saber cut across the corner of his mouth.

From Australia we went to France, which is just across the street. It is a large white marble palace and there we stayed for two hours and a half, walking and looking all the time and it seemed only a few minutes. There are lovely gowns and hats and shoes and gloves for women, men's shirts and shoes and gloves and suspenders, the most beautiful fabrics (cloth of different kinds) that could be imagined.

There are world-famous paintings and statues. There are wonderful old tapestries, each of which covers an entire wall. Rose and I estimated that some of the larger ones were fifty by seventy-five feet. Imagine a picture of that size drawn by a famous artist and then woven thread by thread of the most beautiful colors in the softest tones and all mellowed by time. They are most wonderful. The coloring of the flesh of people, the colors in the sky, and trees and grass, horses, birds and beasts, water and land, all perfect and never fading. Some of them were made in Brussels, the capital in Belgium, that the Germans have now. There was an old hand-carved and gilded bedstead and the body of an old carriage made 500 years ago when Louis XIV was king of France. There were wonderfully made cabinets of brass inlaid with silver and beautiful old furniture and carpets made for Louis XIV. I can not tell you of all but I am bringing a catalog and I will go over it with you.

I think they have paid a fine compliment to the U.S. in some of their exhibits. They have a bronze statue of the "Minute Man of 1776," the American revolutionary soldier, you know. I recognized him the minute I saw him, and nearby there is a small booth filled with personal belongings of General Lafayette, who fought with Washington, you remember. There is a desk and chair he used to use, a couple of his swords crossed, a lamp and inkhorn, his very own old cocked hat that he used to wear and it looks exactly like the pictures we used to see. There is a portrait of him, and one of General Washington and the other French general who helped us.

Oh, I must tell you of the wonderful ropes and strings of pearls, white and pink and black. Then there were some individual pearls, both white and black, as large as a quail's egg.*

There is one little long room. As we came to the archway opening into it and looked down we saw on each side large paintings of battle scenes where the French and Germans were fighting in the old war. There were cities burning, with men fighting in the streets. Generals on horseback leading the cavalry in.

* About three fourths of an inch long.

Pictures of this kind were on all the length of the walls until near the farther end. There, on each side, was a painting of Christ crucified, the only pictures of the kind I ever saw that were not horrible. These were wonderful. Between them in the center of the room was a bronze statue of Sorrow, a woman weeping. The most realistic thing. It almost made me cry to look at it. At the end of the room, covering the whole end wall with the Christ on each side and the weeping woman before it, was a painting of the armies of France. It was a camp at night with a little sentinel fire at one side. The rifles were stacked in a long row down the picture, growing smaller and smaller in the distance. The flag was rolled and resting across the tops of the rifles nearby and the soldiers all lay wrapped in their blankets sleeping. Dawn was just breaking along the skyline and on the clouds rolling away rode the "Phantom Armies of France," the ghosts, I think, of all men and horses who have ever been killed in all the wars of France. The whole picture was the most wonderful lifelike thing I have ever seen and the whole room was a shrine of sorrow.

From France we went to Belgium, which is an annex of the French Building and filled with what poor Belgium could gather up from the wreck. There is a relief map, a model of the city of Brussels, and some beautiful old paintings, and the statues of King Albert and Queen Elizabeth in white marble, looking exactly like those good pictures of them we have in the Metropolitan. After we saw Belgium we went to the Food Products Building, got a couple of Scotch scones and then went to the East Indian tea room in the same building and got some tea and cakes to eat with the scones and sat and rested a few minutes.*

Then we went back and after taking another look at the kangaroos we went into the New Zealand Building where they show moving pictures of the country and people. Do you remember when we had a notion of going to New Zealand before we went to Florida? It is surely a great country. The pictures showed harvesting grain in the hills, too rough for machinery, cut with a sickle,

* This may be where Laura bought the intricately carved cabinet.

bound by hand and threshed with a flail. They showed a harvest where the ground is just a gentle rolling country. There were four harvesters in the field and the grain was fine. The grain was hauled from the field and threshed before our eyes.

We saw also the loading on ships at the docks of oysters, hemp, cheese, wool, and frozen mutton. There were pictures of the great sheep herds and the sheep dogs and shepherds and hundreds and hundreds of sheep. We saw them made to swim through the tanks and we saw them sheared. Also we saw the ugly native islanders that used to be the cannibal tribes in Australia and New Zealand. We saw also the hot-water lake and the steaming cliffs. Believe me, I would stay far from it. The high rock cliffs are pouring hot water into the hot lake from springs all around it and wherever the springs come out of the rocks or the water splashes on them clouds of steam rise. A boat loaded with people went out on the hot-water lake amidst the steam and went around it. The water was so hot they could not put their hands in—one tried and burned himself. There were the hot springs and geysers in another place too, and then pictures of surf bathing on the ocean beach where the people stood away out with boards in their hands and as the waves came in dropped down and rode their boards in.

When we were through here we went down to the Marina, which is the walk along the shore, and saw the gray battleships and the ferries and the ships and boats they were trimming up for the landing of Columbus in the evening, and then home through the lovely courts to an entrance gate where we took the streetcar. We were too late to go out to the battleship as we had intended and so that is left for the next day.

Why! I told you why I changed the address. Mail that comes to the *Bulletin* for us is sent upstairs to Bessie Beatty's office and thrown down on a desk among a pile of papers and there are five careless people there to paw it over, and I did not get your letter enclosing the one from Wilhelm, so I sent you the house address where we live which is 1019 B. Vallejo St., San Francisco.

Lovingly,
Bessie

———

Rose wrote a note to Almanzo which she enclosed with her mother's letter of October 14.

Papa Dear—

Something is happening which I think you should know, though to me, especially, it is a painful subject to contemplate. I notice Mama Bess says nothing about it in her letters, but I can quite understand why she does not. Still, I feel it is only right you should know, and think it my duty to tell you.

Mama Bess is growing fat.

I do not know whether or not it is the fish she eats. She eats a tremendous amount of it. Yet, fish is supposed to be good brain food. I never heard that it was fattening.

Perhaps it is the Scotch scones. They are very delicious, crumbly, hot cakes, spread thick with butter and jam. She eats two of them without a quiver. Once she ate three. Afterward she said she felt queer, and wondered if she had eaten something. It may be the scones.

I will not take her to the scone booth again. It is always a dangerous undertaking anyway, because it is just beside the fish exhibit, and she stands outside the glass cases, looking at the trout and salmon and rock cod and flounders and sand dabs and catfish and ratfish and crabs and shrimps and sea cucumbers and sole, and I am in mortal terror every minute that she will not be able to restrain herself any longer, but will break the glass and eat some of them right there. Even with two scones and a package of Pan-pak and fifteen cents worth of salted nuts and a rosecake and a bag of Saratoga chips in her hand, she still looks at the fish with the same longing expression.

No, I shall not take her to the scone booth any more. I shall go myself, and bring the scones out. Or leave her standing by the big guns where they pop the rice. Ever eat popped rice? It's better than popcorn. Gillette eats it with butter and salt, the same way.

Mama Bess has just interrupted—I am supposed to be writing the "Behind the Headlights" story—she has just interrupted and said, "Luncheon is served." When she cooks the luncheon it's so delicious you can't help overeating. I fear by the time you get this she will be still fatter.

Anyway, I've done my duty and told you.

Lots of Love,
Rose

———

And then Rose had to write again.

San Francisco
October 20, 1915

Dear Papa—

I meant to write you sooner, and hope you have not been worried by not getting a letter from Mama Bess. She was hurt by a streetcar last week but is all right now. She does not want anyone in Mansfield to know about it, because she says it looks as if she could not take care of herself in a city, but on account of not writing for so long she thought I had better write and tell you.

It was not her fault at all. She was going down town with Gillette, and he jumped off the car while it was going full speed. She stood up suddenly, surprised by the way he did, and fell off. The back of her head struck the stone pavement, and things looked pretty bad for awhile, but they got her to a hospital right away and the doctor said there was no danger, it was only a superficial wound, no fracture or anything like that. She is coming home today.

It has been too bad, because she has lost a whole week and it will probably be another before she can get around and see much. We will not be able to get anything from the streetcar company because it was not their fault at all.

She has been in the best hospital in town, and except for a bad headache she has been quite comfortable. Of course she is pretty weak yet, from the shock and all, but that will be gone in a few days more. She had written you a long letter, and had it in her hand when the accident occurred. We can not find it, and suppose it has been mailed to you all right by someone who picked it up. It had a note in it from me, so you will know by that whether or not you got it.

She has an order for several articles from the [Missouri] *Ruralist*, and she will get them this next week and we will write them up. That will be some real money for her.

I did not read her your first letter about not being well until the second came that said you were better. I hope you're feeling fine by this time; when I read the first letter I certainly felt blue.

She told me what to tell you to feed the hens, and I wrote it down on a sheet of hospital paper. I will send it with this.

She says she supposes there is no use feeding them much if they are getting so much corn, she says probably that is the reason they are not laying, because they get too much corn, which is not good to make them lay, and they have so much of that they do not eat things that would make them lay.

It certainly has been too bad, that she was needed at home so much. She is always worrying about how you are getting along and it is a shame I could not have had a little more money so you could have a man and someone to cook for you, both. But I suppose even then you would not find her cooking as good as yours by a long ways.

I am writing the life of Henry Ford* now, and he was telling me yesterday that he is building a farm tractor now that sells for $200 and weighs only 1,500 pounds. It runs for eleven hours on fifty-four cents worth of kerosene. It is not on the market yet, but will be, soon, and it struck me it would be better than a team of horses for lots of the farm work, because it would not cost any more, and when it was not working it would not be eating, and you could make it go fast or slow just as you liked. I am going to ask him more about it.

I am going down to the hospital now to get Mama Bess and bring her out to the house. She said to tell you, whatever you did, to take good care of yourself and Inky till she gets back. She says she thinks she ought to start pretty soon, on account of your being there with all the work to do, but my private opinion

* The story was part of a series for the *Bulletin*. In 1917 it was published in book form as *Henry Ford's Own Story*, as told to Rose Wilder Lane.

is that she's homesick. I want her to see a little more of the state, Petaluma, and some of Marin County, though, before she leaves. It is hard to show her as much as I would like to because I have to keep on earning my little pay envelope, and that takes a lot of time.

Lots and lots of love,
Rose

———

ENCLOSURE:

Mama says, about the hens—if you have not already mixed up the package of fenugreek that is on the end of the long shelves near the woodshed door—mix it up with the package of cayenne pepper that is on the shelf beside it, and the same quantity of ginger, then add lime until it is the right color—she says you know what color it should be.

Feed it the same as Pratts food—about two tablespoons to a dishpan of feed.

For their morning mess feed them as much mash as they will eat up *clean* in twenty minutes—don't feed them any more than that.

Recipe for morning mash:

4 measures bran

2 measures corn chop (fine ground chop is
    best)

1 measure cut bone

½ measure linseed meal

If you think they need more lime, put more in the feed—maybe a couple of tablespoons in a feed. And do not forget the salt.

———

San Francisco
October 22, 1915

Manly Dear,

I am so sorry you have been sick and that Inky hurt himself. Rose says she wrote you that I got hurt. I am all right, only a little weak yet. I had thought by this time I would have everything done and be ready to start home. I know I should be there helping you get things ready for winter unless by some good chance you were making things ready without me, but I might have known that you would not be able to get help if you particularly wanted it.

At last I have a letter from the *Ruralist* with orders for copy and recommendations that give me passes into the Fair and throws the whole Missouri part of it wide open to me. It is a shame they could not have sent it sooner and I do not understand why they did not. The men in charge of the Missouri exhibits want me to persuade the *Ruralist* to issue a special edition on Missouri at the P.P.I.E. [Panama Pacific International Exposition] and I have wired them about it. If they tell me to go ahead with it I will have my hands full for a few days getting out the copy for the whole paper. I expect to hear from them tomorrow. If I do the special edition I will not be able to start for home before ten days, but if I just write the articles I already have the orders for I expect to start for home in a week from now.*

I have given up the idea of the ocean trip. It would break into Rose's work and she is

* Laura did write the lead story for a spread on the Missouri exhibits at the Fair, which appeared the day after the P.P.I.E. closed—December 5, 1915. And she wrote another article about food at the Fair, with recipes, which is condensed as an Appendix.

very busy. I would not care to go alone and it would cost more than to come straight home. So I will take the train here for Kansas City without change. I am also going to let the trip to Petaluma go. I would rather spend the time at the Fair, save the expense and the tiresome train ride, and get all the information I want from the experts at the poultry exhibit here.

So you see I have mapped out for myself the work for the *Ruralist*, a couple of Sunday stories for the [St. Louis] Post Dispatch, learning what I can at the poultry exhibit here, a day on the battleship *Oregon* already arranged for, and then home. Perhaps you think it has taken me longer than it should have to make my visit but you have no idea how confusing this great city of San Francisco was to me and how a very little of the crowds and the streets tired me. Rose has been very busy too and because of that we could not always do as we would have liked to do.

I have accomplished some of the things that I came to do to my entire satisfaction and some are still up in the air. Stine has been out of town ever since I have been here so that we have been unable to find out anything definite about that $250 or any more to stop [mortgage] interest with, but Rose will try again within a day or two. I did so want to bring it home with me but if I can not do that it will come later. Gillette is working extra now with fair prospect of a regular job next week. If he gets it things will be smoothed out considerably.

Rose got into the movies again, unknown to her until it was all over. She was taken with the Henry Ford party on board the battleship *Oregon*. She is working now on the life of Ford, which will begin soon in the *Bulletin*. I do not know whether the outlaw story will be published in book form or not. If you are reading Rose's story of the engineer you may like to know that every incident in it is true. She went all around hunting up engineers to talk with and she found one that fired on an engine through Dakota north of us during the long winter,* or rather did not fire, because the trains could not run. In that part of the

* See *The Long Winter*, which Laura wrote over twenty years later, about her girlhood in De Smet, Dakota (now South Dakota).

story Rose used some of what he told her and some that I told her.

Rose and Gillette are out chasing around after Ford to get more material for Rose's story (it being Sunday Gillette is not working). I would be with them, only I am not quite strong enough yet. I am going to the Fair tomorrow and do some of the Missouri work in a motor chair like the one they pictured Steve with once.

Oh, I know Millman, who draws Steve. He is a fine young fellow, red-headed and with a funny quirk to the corner of his lips when he smiles and simply delightful in a clean, wholesome way. To show his sympathy for me because I got hurt he is going to give me an original drawing of Steve—the pen and ink picture that he made himself and that the pictures in the paper are made from.

Do take care of yourself and Inky and whisper to him that I will be there before long. I have so many nice things planned to do when I do get home and I am sure the woods are beautiful. I love the city of San Francisco. It is beautiful but I would not give one Ozark hill for all the rest of the state that I have seen. Oh, by the way, Missouri has SHOWN THEM at the P.P.I.E. Carried off more prizes than any state except California and beat California on mines.

Do not expect to get any more long letters from me for I will be so busy doing all the writing I can for the papers and getting things wound up so I can start home that I will not have time. Nor do I think I should spend the time writing when I can be seeing more things and tell you about them all when I come.

I must stop now and rest a little for I am tired.

Goodbye for this time,
Lovingly, Bessie

APPENDIX

MAGIC IN PLAIN FOODS

An article (condensed) by Laura which appeared in the [Missouri] Ruralist *on November 20, 1915.*

T he thought came to me, while I wandered among the exhibits in the Food Products Building at the San Francisco Exposition, that Aladdin with his wonderful lamp had no more power than the modern woman in her kitchen. She takes down the receiver to telephone her grocery order, and immediately all over the world the monstrous genii of machinery are obedient to her command. All the nations of the world bring their offerings to her door—fruits from South America, Hawaii, Africa; tea and spices from India, China and Japan; olives and oil from Italy; coffee from strange tropical islands; sugar from Cuba and the Philippines.

This modern magic works both ways. The natives of all these far away places may eat the flour made from the wheat growing in the fields outside our kitchen windows. I never shall look at Missouri wheat fields again without thinking of the "Breads of All Nations" exhibit, where natives of eight foreign nations, in the national costumes, were busy making the breads of their countries from our own American flour.

We use raisins, flour, tea, breakfast food, and a score of other common things without a thought of the modern miracles that make it possible for us to have them.

One has a greater feeling of respect for the flour used daily, after seeing the infinite pains taken to turn out the perfect article. From the time the wheat is poured into the hoppers until, in our kitchens, we cut the string that ties the sack, the flour is not exposed to the outer air. It is not touched by human hands until we dip the flour sifter into it.

Ten years ago, too, we seeded our raisins by hand ourselves, or bribed the children to the task by giving them a share to eat. Today we buy seeded raisins in boxes, without giving a thought to how the seeding is done. You may be sure of this—these package raisins are clean. They are scientifically clean, sterilized by steam and packed hot. In the Food Products Building I saw these machines at work. This is the process:

Sun-dried Muscat grapes are stemmed by machinery, then sent through 26 feet of live steam at 212 pounds pressure. From this they fall onto a steel, sawtooth cylinder, and pass under three soft rubber rolls which crush the raisin and loosen the seeds. They then strike a corrugated steel roll which throws out the seeds. The raisin passes on, is lifted from the cylinder by a steel rake and dropped into paraffin-paper-lined boxes, which are closed while the raisins are still hot from the steam sterilizing.

Space forbids that I should describe the

scores of exhibits in this enormous [Food Products] building devoted to the preparation of different foods, a task which always has been considered woman's work. I can only briefly mention the Japanese rice cakes—tiny bits of paste half an inch long and no thicker than paper. The smiling Oriental in charge drops them into boiling olive oil, and they puff into delicious looking brown rolls three inches long. They look as toothsome as a homemade doughnut, but to your wild amazement, when you bite them there is nothing there.

I must say one word about the rose cakes: delicious cakes baked in the form of a rose, and as good as they are beautiful. And I am sure nobody leaves the Exposition without speaking of the Scotch scones; everybody eats them who can reach them. They are baked by a Scotchman from Edinburgh, who turns out more than 4,000 of them daily. They are buttered, spread with jam, and handed over the counter as fast as four girls can do it. And the counter is surrounded by a surging mob all day long.

As I went from booth to booth, they gave

me samples of the breads they had made, with our American flour—the little, bland Chinese girl in her bright blue pajama costume, the smiling high-cheeked Russian peasant girl, the Hindoo in his gay turban, the swarthy, black-eyed Mexican—all of them eager to have me like their national foods. And I must say I did like most of it so well that I brought the recipes away with me, and pass them on to you:

Russian Forrest

One pound flour, yolks of 3 eggs, 1 whole egg, ½ cup milk. Mix well and knead very thoroughly. Cut in pieces size of walnuts; roll very, very thin. Cut the center in strips, braid together and fry in deep fat. Drain, and sprinkle with powdered sugar.

Mexican Tamale Loaf

One pound veal, 1 onion, 2 cloves of garlic, 1 tablespoon chili powder, 1 can tomatoes (strained), 24 green olives (chopped). Boil the meat until very tender, take from the broth, cool and chop. Return to the broth, add salt to taste, add the onion and garlic chopped fine, then the tomatoes, olives and chili powder. Let all come to the boiling point, then add enough yellow cornmeal to make as thick as mush, turn into molds and set aside to cool. The loaf may be served either cold or sliced and fried.

German Honey Cake

One cup honey, molasses or syrup; ½ cup sugar, 2 cups flour, 1 teaspoon cinnamon, 1 teaspoon cloves, 1 teaspoon ginger, 2 teaspoons baking powder. Beat honey and sugar 20 minutes, then add the spices, the baking powder, and lastly the flour. Pour into well-buttered baking sheets and bake 15 minutes in a moderate oven. Cover with chocolate icing and cut in squares.

Italian White Tagliarini

Three cups flour, ½ cup hot water, 2 eggs, 1 teaspoon salt. Mix and knead thoroughly, roll very thin as for noodles, and cut in any desired shape. Allow to dry 1 hour and cook in boiling water for 10 minutes, drain, and serve with sauce.

Sauce for Tagliarini

One-half cup olive oil, 1 large pod garlic, 1 large carrot, 1 large can tomatoes, salt and pepper, 2 large onions, 5 stalks celery, 1 cup parsley, ½ pound hamburg steak, ⅛ teaspoon cloves, ½ cup butter. Heat the oil in an iron skillet or kettle, then add onions and garlic chopped fine. Cook until transparent but not brown, then add the rest of the ingredients chopped fine. Cook slowly for 2 hours.

Croissants (French Crescents)

Four cups flour, 1 cup warm water, 1 cake compressed yeast, ½ teaspoon salt, 1 cup butter. Sift and measure the flour into a bowl, add the yeast which has been dissolved in the water, then the salt. Mix and knead thoroughly. Let rise 2 or 3 hours, then roll out 1 inch thick and lay the butter on the center. Fold the dough over and roll out four times as for puff paste, then cut in pieces as for finger rolls, having the ends thinner than the middles. Form in crescent shape, brush with egg, and bake in a moderate oven.

Chinese Almond Cakes

Four cups flour, 1 cup lard, 1½ cups sugar, 1 egg, ½ teaspoon baking powder. Mix and knead thoroughly. Take off pieces of dough the size of an English walnut, roll in a smooth round ball, then flatten about half. Make a depression on the top and place in it 1 almond. Place on pans, 2 inches apart, and bake a golden brown.

LAURA INGALLS WILDER was born in 1867 in the log cabin described in *Little House in the Big Woods*. As her classic Little House books tell us, she and her family traveled by covered wagon across the Midwest. She and her husband, Almanzo Wilder, made their own covered-wagon trip with their daughter, Rose, to Mansfield, Missouri. There Laura wrote her story in the Little House books, and lived until she was ninety years old. For millions of readers, however, she lives forever as the little pioneer girl in the beloved Little House books.

ROSE WILDER LANE was born in 1886 to Almanzo and Laura Ingalls Wilder. Like her mother, she was a prolific writer, and is the author of works of both fiction and nonfiction, including the best-selling *Let the Hurricane Roar*. She died in 1968.

ROGER LEA MacBRIDE was born in New York State and is a graduate of Harvard Law School. He is the author or editor of nine books, including *Little House on Rocky Ridge* and *Little Farm in the Ozarks*, the first two books in the Rocky Ridge Years series, which continues the story of Laura, Almanzo, and Rose Wilder. He lives in Miami Beach, Florida.

MARGOT PATTERSON DOSS, author of *San Francisco at Your Feet* among other books and for 30 years a columnist for the San Francisco *Chronicle*, is also a member of the Citizens' Advisory Commission to the Golden Gate National Recreation Area, which now includes the place where Laura enjoyed the Exposition in 1915.